FIBERGLASS REPAIRS

Examples of Fiberglass Structures.

FIBERGLASS REPAIRS

A Guide to Fiberglass/Polyester Repairs on Boats, Cars,
Snowmobiles and Other Structures

PAUL J. PETRICK

CORNELL MARITIME PRESS

Centreville, Maryland

Library of Congress Cataloging-in-Publication Data

Petrick, Paul J   1921-
   Fiberglass repairs.

   1. Fiberglass boats—Maintenance and repair.
2. Glass fibers. 3. Polyesters. I. Title.
VM321.P38   623.82'07'38   76-17811
ISBN 0-87033-222-8

Manufactured in the United States of America
First edition, 1976; sixth printing, 1994

CONTENTS

The author's tractor drifted down the hill when the parking brakes failed to hold; and the front end loader poked through the side of the boat (which was parked on a trailer next to the barn) and pushed it through the block wall of the barn. It left a hole large enough to crawl through. This happened about 15 years ago. We repaired the boat, making it stronger than it was originally; and it is still in service today.

ACKNOWLEDGMENTS

I am grateful to John Holter and Bob Walter for photographic assistance and to the Owens Corning Fiberglas® Corporation and Columbia Yacht, a Division of Whittaker Corporation, Chesapeake, Virginia, for supplying the photographs used on the cover and frontispiece.

P.J.P.

INTRODUCTION

There is virtually no damage to a fiberglass boat, car body, or any other fiberglass-reinforced laminate, regardless of how severe, which cannot be completely repaired and made even stronger than the original product. During the last 23 years we have repaired boats which were crushed by falling trees, damaged by collisions with front end loaders, involved in auto accidents when trailered, damaged by fire, or battered by storms and hurricanes. Surprisingly enough, the structural repairs are easier to accomplish and less tedious than the cosmetic repairs. All that is required is common sense and the ability to work with hand tools. This manual provides all of the technical information needed and is written in layman's language.

RECOMMENDED SUPPLIES

The following supplies are those which are customarily kept on hand for fiberglass repair work. All of them will not be required for individual jobs; after reading the text and studying the procedures, you will be able to determine which ones are necessary for your specific project. The same, of course, pertains to the list of tools and equipment which follows.

1. Fiberglass, resins, catalyst, and acetone
2. Sandpaper (abrasive papers) in sheet and disc forms
   - 36 grit (open grit) for very coarse sanding
   - 80 grit for general coarse sanding
   - 150 grit for medium sanding
   - 240 grit wet dry for fine sanding
   - 400 and 600 grit wet dry for very fine sanding
   - Rubbing and polishing compound for final polishing
   - A good grade of boat or automotive wax
3. Masking tape
4. Clear elastic food wrapping plastic film
5. Small paper mixing cups (not Styrofoam) and mixing sticks
6. Eye dropper
7. Dust mask and goggles for coarse power sanding
8. Inexpensive paint brushes
9. Paper towels or old rags (not rayon)

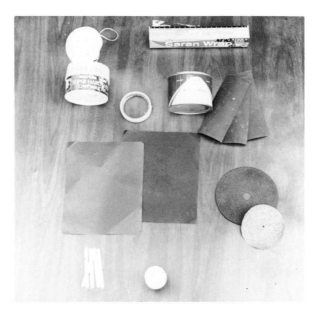

Recommended supplies.

RECOMMENDED TOOLS

1. Combination disc/sander/polisher or separate high-speed disc sander and low-speed disc polisher
2. Saber saw with metal cutting blades
3. ¼" electric drill (preferably variable speed)
4. Lamb's wool buffing pad
5. Swivel or flex head rubber sanding disc for ¼" electric drill
6. Abrasive or carbide grinding burrs
7. Sanding block
8. Narrow and wide putty knives
9. Vibrator sander
10. Utility knife
11. Scissors
12. Heat gun or heat lamps for cold weather applications

Recommended tools.

FIBERGLASS REPAIRS

Typical totaled hull and deck stove in by a falling tree. It is typical of repair that can be made with polyester and fiberglass.

1.

FIBERGLASS

Fiberglass, like polyesters, is available in many different forms, but for our purposes we will concentrate on only three: 1) Woven fiberglass boat cloth; 2) Fiberglass matt; and 3) Fiberglass woven roving.

The fiberglass content in a laminate determines the ultimate tensile strength of the laminate. For example, a laminate with a 50% fiberglass and 50% resin content (by weight) will be much stronger than a laminate consisting of 25% fiberglass and 75% resin. Fiberglass reinforcement acts similarly to tie rods in concrete. Without it the resin would be very brittle and have a tendency to crack or rupture.

Woven Fiberglass Fabric (Boat Cloth)

As can be seen from the photograph, this is a simple woven fabric made from twisted fiberglass filaments. Technically, it is usually a 10 oz. fabric (weight 10 oz. per sq. yd.) and is a 16 x 16 construction (having 16 strands per inch). To be readily compatible with polyesters, it should have a chrome or volan finish, which means it is shiny in appearance. Dull looking fabrics should be avoided, as they are generally "unfinished" and do not "wet out" with the polyester resin as readily or as completely. When used with polyesters, woven cloth produces the strongest boat laminates—generally having a 45—50% glass to resin ratio. Having a high glass content, the laminates produced using all woven fabric are usually more flexible than laminates produced with, for example, fiberglass matt which would have a much lower glass content.

Fiberglass fabric, unlike most other woven materials, has a slip weave which allows the 90 degree threads to readily slip or slide over one another. For this reason, woven fiberglass (fabric or woven roving) will allow the individual strands to slip and rearrange themselves so that the fabric will conform to compound curves in one piece without slitting.

To cut fiberglass woven fabric or woven roving from a roll, to assure a straight 90 degree cut, pull and remove one strand from side to side from the width and cut along the line left by the missing strand.

Woven Roving

This is a very coarse woven material generally made from 60 filament end continuous roving weighing 24 oz. per sq. yd. It is much thicker than woven boat fabric, and therefore produces a much thicker ply of

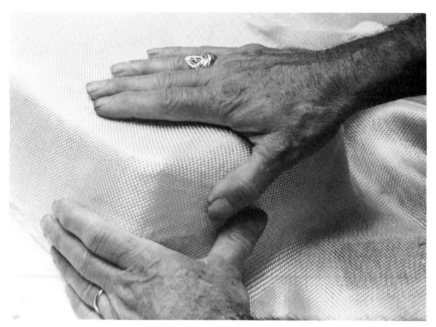

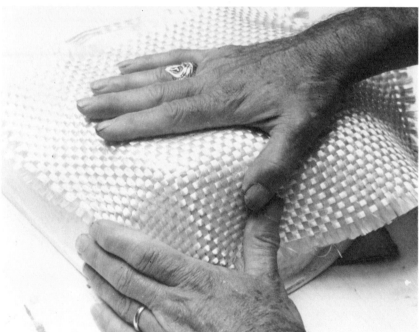

(Top) Woven fiberglass boat cloth. Note how the cloth will configurate to compound curves due to its "weave slip." (Bottom) Woven roving. Although much coarser than boat cloth, the weave will also "slip," allowing it to configurate to compound curves.

laminate than the boat cloth. Very little strength is sacrificed with woven roving yielding a laminate generally of 45% glass to resin ratio. It is almost always used as an alternate layer with matt to yield the best adhesion and combination tensile strength and stiffness. In repair work, if woven roving is to be used, it is always best to begin and end with matt, with woven roving between each layer of matt.

Fiberglass Matt

This is a feltlike material made from chopped strands of fiberglass filaments, pressed into a matt form and held together with a resin soluble binder. It is available in various thicknesses, generally ranging from ¾ oz. to 3 oz. per sq. ft. (Note: The ounce designation for matt is

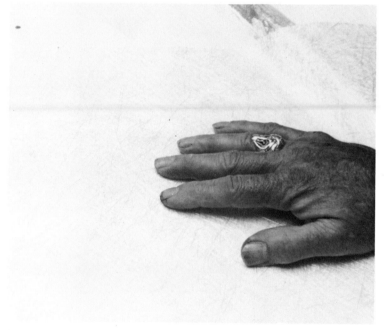

Fiberglass matt. When dry, it is stiff and will not configurate to compound curves; when wetted with resin, it will.

per square foot, whereas that for woven fabric and woven roving is per square yard.) One- and two-ounce are the most common and readily available through the marine outlets. Matt in its unwetted state is generally fairly stiff, and will not configure to a compound curve. However, when wetted out with polyester resin, the resin soluble binder holding it together dissolves; and then the matt will behave and configure to various shapes and compound curves.

Matt yields the weakest laminate—with a ratio ranging from 25—35% glass per resin. It does have its advantages, as it also yields the stiffest laminate, and has the best inter laminate bonding strength due to its non-woven (nondirectional) pattern.

In boat manufacture, it is a general practice to use alternate layers of matt and woven roving, as this combination assures excellent inter laminate bond, sufficient stiffness, and sufficient tensile strength. In repair work, matt and woven fabric (with the matt always being applied first) are generally used instead of matt and woven roving. Either combination can be used, but considering that woven fabric is generally more readily available than woven roving, fabric is generally the more popular choice. Woven roving, on the other hand, produces a much thicker laminate, almost as strong as woven fabric, and in one operation. The choice is up to the individual.

POLYESTER RESINS

Polyester resins come in hundreds of different formulations, but we are concerned with only a few in boat repairing. The polyesters which we will deal with are liquid plastics to which a liquid catalyst (MEK peroxide) is added and which causes them to cure into a hard solid state, whether in a thin film or a large mass. They, unlike paints, will cure when completely covered without exposure to air.

The four types which we will deal with in boat repairing are: 1) Air-inhibited clear lay-up resin; 2) Clear non-air-inhibited coating resin; 3) Pigmented gel coat; and 4) Polyester putty.

Air-Inhibited Clear Lay-Up Resin

Air-inhibited simply means a resin which cures with a tacky upper surface when exposed to the air. It must be remembered that only the uppermost surface will remain tacky. If this resin were catalyzed and applied to a polished mold or a piece of cellophane or Saran Wrap®, and after it cured, peeled from that surface, the upper portion would be tacky and the lower surface would be hard and tack-free. Air-inhibited resins are used in order to achieve a true molecular bond between cured coats or laminates, regardless of how much time has elapsed. This is most necessary, because in many instances laminates are made in stages involving several days or weeks. It is virtually impossible to sand the tacky upper surfaces of an air-inhibited resin without gumming up the sandpaper. Quite a few pieces of sandpaper would have to be used and discarded before getting down to the hard, non-tacky portion.

Non-Air-Inhibited Resin

This is called a surfacing resin and is the most readily available resin through marine outlets. It contains a waxy type of additive, which floats to the surface when applied and forms a thin film to prevent the air from coming in contact with the liquid resin surface during curing. This resin cures to a tack-free surface and is ideal for sanding and polishing, as it will not gum up the sandpaper. One exception is if this resin is applied to hot surfaces or if it is allowed to get hot while curing. The waxy additive that creates the protective barrier against the air has a melting point of about 100°F. If the applied coating exceeds this temperature during curing, the surfacing additive melts and becomes ineffective. This would not deter it from curing normally, except that the uppermost surface would remain tacky like an air-inhibited resin.

Saran Wrap® is a registered trademark of Dow Chemical Co.

When using a tack-free resin, it must be thoroughly sanded to assure a good intercoat bond, if another coat is to be applied over it.

Pigmented Gel Coats

This is the polyester formula which the boat manufacturer applies to his polished female mold prior to proceeding with his subsequent fiberglass lay-up. When the boat is removed from the female mold, the pigmented gel coat represents the exterior colored surface of the hull or deck. It is also the layer of pigmented polyester which acts as a barrier between the fiberglass reinforcement and the elements to achieve good weather, chemical, and abuse resistance. Fiberglass filaments, although very strong, being in fiber form, do have a wicking action, and would present a very poor surface to be exposed to the elements. It is for this reason that a gel coat should always be used on exterior surfaces, and surfacing coatings should be used on the rougher interior surfaces. Gel coats are always air-inhibited, so that the surface away from the mold will remain tacky and permit a true molecular bond to exist between it and the succeeding coats of resin and fiberglass. Gel coats are generally more thixotropic (a two-dollar word meaning thicker in consistency so that they can be applied in heavy thicknesses on a vertical surface without running or draining). Their thixotropic nature makes them unsuitable for wetting out fiberglass. They are also generally pigmented, as this color pigment represents the final color of the boat exterior.

Polyester Putty

This is simply a polyester resin to which fillers such as clay or talc are added in sufficient quantities to convert them into a putty consistency. This putty consistency allows them to be troweled or knifed into a gouge or void, and stay put without draining until they have cured. They can be made by adding sufficient quantities of filler to any of the three previously mentioned materials. They are also available in pre-mixed form through most marine supply houses. There are also many brands available through automotive supply houses as "body patching compounds." If buying a premixed putty, make certain that it has a polyester—not an epoxy—base, as the epoxy based materials will not permit the succeeding polyesters to attain a good inter coat bond.

Sometimes the automotive type fillers utilize a paste rather than a liquid catalyst. It is only necessary to follow the directions on the can.

All of the above polyesters can be intermixed. For example, pigmented gel coat can be mixed with the putties or other resins to lend color to them if desired. Also, small amounts of putty can be added to pigmented gel coat to come up with a fairly accurate color match for filling small scratches and light gouges in a thicker-than-gel-coat consistency that will not run.

Converting Air-Inhibited Resins to Non-Air-Inhibited Resins

If you have an air-inhibited resin which you would like to apply as a surface coat to cure to a non-tacky hard finish, it is normally accomplished by adding 1% "surfacing additive." This, however, is impractical in many instances, as surfacing additive is a highly specialized material which is only available through a few commercial plastic supply houses. This makes it extremely difficult for the average person to obtain.

Surfacing additive is essentially household wax or paraffin diluted and melted in styrene—another almost inaccessible material. With the following procedure, styrene is not necessary.

Purchase a small box of canning wax—this is enough to convert an entire drum of resin, as it takes only a minute trace of wax (1/10 of 1%) to form the necessary waxy film which allows the resin to cure tack-free. This would work out to about one gram of wax per quart of resin. Household wax generally comes in small bars one-half inch thick. If you take a razor blade or sharp penknife and cut off a 3/8″ x 3/8″ x ½″ square, it will weigh just about one gram—sufficient to treat one quart of resin.

Take this small cube of wax and shave it into very fine flakes—the smaller the better.

Take about one-half pint of resin from the quart to be treated, and pour it into a small tin can or glass jar. Add the shaved wax to the half pint of resin. In order to dissolve the wax into the resin, the resin must be warmed to exceed the melting point of the wax. When this is done, the wax will go into solution with the resin, and stay in solution.

To heat the half pint of resin, bring a small pot of water to a boil, remove it from the stove, and set the bottom of the can or jar into the hot water, thus creating your own double boiler.

Make certain that no water gets into the resin. While holding the can in the hot water, stir the resin constantly with a small mixing stick until the wax dissolves and goes into solution. This will be easy to see, as the flakes of wax will float on top of the resin until they are melted and dissolved. This whole process takes only a few minutes. When all of the wax is dissolved in the warm half pint, pour this concentrate back into the quart can and stir all of the resin together to disperse the wax throughout the entire quart.

Caution: Never heat the resin directly on the stove as it will get too hot and would easily catch on fire. In cold weather all of the resin should be at room temperature (at least 70° F.) at the beginning. Also remember that immediately after treatment the resin will be quite a bit above room temperature and this will greatly shorten your pot life when catalyzed, if used immediately. Resin thus treated can be stored and used at any time afterwards, the same as any other resin.

3.

CATALYST AND CURING

INITIATOR

The catalyst is an oxidizing agent (MEK peroxide) which, when dispersed into the polyester resin, causes it to polymerize (another two-dollar word) and change from a liquid to a solid. As previously mentioned, this will happen in a thin film or a heavy mass. There are many different concentrations of catalyst, and there are also various reactivities in different polyesters which cause some to cure faster than others when the same amount of catalyst is added. Most typical "boat" resins sold in marine outlets require approximately one percent catalyst to effect a polyester cure in 30 to 45 minutes. The catalyst is usually packaged in ½ oz. bottles (not quite full) which contain 10 cc. This is sufficient to catalyze one quart (2—2¼ lbs. of resin). Catalyzed resin will always cure or gel faster in the container in which it is mixed than in the thin film or laminate. This is because the reaction of the catalyst with the polyester causes a mild heat which readily builds up in the mass of the container but which dissipates when the polyester is applied in a thinner film.

If the polyester were catalyzed and left in the container, this heat (exotherm) could build up to 200° or 300°F. and actually cause smoking. This seldom happens, as the polyester is generally used and not left to harden in a large mass. If it does happen, pouring water on top of the mass will cool it down sufficiently to stop the smoking; but of course the resin will be useless.

Catalyst can be added in varying amounts from ½—5% to expedite the gel time, the working life (pot life), and the cure time. One-half percent catalyst will generally yield a one hour pot life, 1% a 30-minute pot life and 2% a 15-minute pot life, etc. Consequently, quicker cures can be achieved by increasing the amount of catalyst added to the polyester. Remember, a quicker surface cure also means a shorter pot life or working time; so only as much polyester should be mixed with catalyst as can be used within a specific time. For very small repairs, small amounts of polyester are catalyzed (down to one teaspoonful) to prevent waste.

Table 1 is a table of small quantities and the catalyst necessary for a 1% mixture. For faster cures doubling the amount of catalyst will double the concentration and render a faster cure.

8

Table 1

Polyester Resin	Catalyst for 1% Solution
1 tsp.	2 drops
1 tbsp.	4 drops
½ pt. (8 oz.)	1/12 oz. or 2½ cc. (100 drops)
1 pt. (16 oz.)	1/6 oz. or 5 cc. (200 drops)
1 qt. (32 oz.)	1/3 oz. or 10 cc. (400 drops)

When mixing very small amounts, it is customary to add 2—3% catalyst to expedite the cure, as pot life is no problem when working with small quantities.

Pot Life vs. Cure Time

In the previous paragraphs we have referred to pot life and cure time. Polyesters, when they proceed to cure, undergo the following changes —when the pot life has expired, they change from a liquid state to rubber cement consistency, a cheese consistency, a hard rubber consistency, a hard rigid consistency, and finally the fully hardened post cured piece. As previously mentioned, various polyesters by various suppliers have different reactivities. Table 2 is a chart of a typical polyester resin for thick laminates.

Table 2

Stage of Cure	Time Elapsed
Pot life with 1% catalyst (liquid state)	0—30 min.
"Rubber cement" consistency (starting to gel)	30—32 min.
"Cheese" consistency (trimming time)	32—40 min.
"Hard rubber" (time to start sanding)	41—60 min.
Hard (hard enough to use)	60 min.
Final post cure (ultimate hardness)	2 weeks

Note: If you wish to trim a laminate with a utility knife or razor blade, it should be done while the laminate is in the "cheese" consistency state. Grinding or sanding can be done any time following this.

Caution: Liquid catalyst is a water-clear, extremely powerful oxidizing agent. Technically it is 60% concentration of Methyl Ethyl Ketone Peroxide in Dimethylphthalate. It should always be kept out of the reach of children. Contact with the skin will not have a severe burning effect such as acids produce (except in tender areas or eyes), but its highly oxidizing nature can cause a slight burning under prolonged exposure. Areas contacted should be flushed with water or washed with soap and water.

Heating to Hasten the Cure

Temperature has a profound effect on the curing rate of polyesters.

Average temperature is considered about 75° F. and the gel times previously given are predicated on that temperature. There is a "Fifteen-Degree Rule" common in the industry that simply states that for each 15-degree increase in temperature over 75° F. the pot life and cure rate is halved; and for each 15 degrees less in temperature, the pot life and cure rate is doubled. For example, if a typical polyester resin has a pot life of 30 minutes with 1% catalyst, then it will have a 15-minute pot life at 90° F., and a 7½-minute pot life at 105° F., etc. Conversely, the same resin will have a pot life of one hour at 60° F. and two hours at 45° F. Polyesters should never be used under 60° F. unless extra catalyst is used or a source of external heat is available.

Several sources of external heat are: portable electric heaters, hair dryers, commercial heat guns, and infrared heat lamps.

It must be remembered that external heat should not be used (over 100° F.) on surfacing resins while they are in the liquid state (refer to the paragraph on surfacing resins) if a tack-free surface is required.

Paste Catalyst

Some polyester auto body patching compounds (putties) are supplied with a paste, rather than a liquid catalyst. Liquid catalysts can be used with them, but the pot life and cure rate will be much quicker. Paste catalyst should never be used with the liquid polyesters calling for liquid catalyst, as the paste would be too low in reactivity and the liquid polyesters would not cure. If this happens inadvertently, then only concentrated external heat for a prolonged time period will cure the resin.

*for high volume application
lower amount of activator
to prevent excessive heat
-very fast cure time

(ex) 5 gal vcam @ 65° = 80 cc of MEKP

#10 coffcan @ 75 = 15 cc MEKP

*styrene & Acetone may swell the same

4.

PIGMENTATION AND COLOR MATCHING

This is the most difficult operation to perform in fiberglass boat repair. In fact, in many instances it is impractical or impossible for the average person (and sometimes professional) to accomplish.

White is generally no, problem. Though there are many shades of white, most boat manufacturers use a pure titanium dioxide white which does not vary greatly in shade. All pigmented polyesters undergo some color change with age—some very slight; others very severe. This depends on the shade of color used and the type of pigments used—whether organic or inorganic. White generally undergoes a slight darkening with age; but the darker colors, particularly the ones manufactured with organic pigments, undergo a severe fading with age.

In professional repairing of fiberglass boats, it is generally a practice to match white repairs, and to completely paint over other colors. Even if you had in your employ a professional color-match chemist, such as we have had for years, for architectural work, color matching of other colors is impractical. Such matching requires an infinite amount of base colors, an infinite amount of patience; and when you are finished, the color to which you matched will change shade in aging and no longer match.

Some boat owners, desperately striving to achieve a color match after exhausting all possibilities in the marine outlets, have tried the "universal" type pigments found in paint stores. These concentrated paste pigments for matching paints are made in a variety of formulations, some of which are compatible with polyesters, and others are not.

An incompatible pigment will cause the polyester to cure incompletely, or in some instances not cure at all. It is strictly a hit-or-miss proposition, and if this route is to be taken, testing is in order.

First, use no more pigment than is absolutely necessary to gain opacity. To make the test, catalyze a small amount of non-air-inhibited resin (tack-free) and divide it in half into two small paper cups. Add the necessary pigment to one cup and leave the other clear. Apply a coating of each to a surface such as a piece of wood using two clean brushes. Leave some materials in the cups so that you can test their cure in a casting as well as a coating. Observe how the two coatings and the two castings cure. If the pigmented coating and casting cure slower than the clear, it indicates that the pigment is having an inhibiting (retarding) effect on the curing process, and the pigment should be held in suspect. If they finally cure to the same hardness, even though the pigmented materials took a little longer, or if they cure at the same rate with the same ultimate hardness, the pigment can be used. If, however, the pigmented version does not cure with the same hardness as the clear, it is incompatible and should not be considered. Test for surface hardness in the coating by using the edge of your thumbnail or a coin to determine the scratch resistance of the coating. On the casting, press a nail point into it with considerable pressure. If the pigmented version "dimples" considerably more than the clear, this indicates an inhibited cure. Final testing should not be made until the samples have aged for at least 24 hours.

In some instances, matched gel coats can be attained through the boat manufacturer, but even then the match cannot be guaranteed.

Fortunately most boats are white, and consequently matching them to a reasonable shade is relatively easy.

Our suggestion on other colors is to contact the manufacturer if practical and determine whether he can supply a matched gel coat. If he can, order a small quantity. Catalyze a teaspoonful and spread it on a piece of waxed glass or plastic wrap. After it has cured, peel the chip from the base to determine how close the color matches. If it is close, depending on your or your customer's approval, you can proceed to match the color of the repair. If it is unacceptable, then do as the professional does—lightly sand and spray the entire area with a good grade of epoxy paint.

Caution: Most paste pigments supplied by marine supply houses are mixed with a liquid plasticizer. When using such pigments, never use any more pigment in the resin than is necessary to provide opacity. Overpigmentation can add too much plasticizer, which could result in a partial, or noncure of the resin—known as total inhibition.

5.

TIPS ON SANDING AND POLISHING

Abrasive papers consist of small particles of abrasive granules glued to a sheet of paper or cloth backing. The size of the particles determines the "grit."

Coarse grit papers are available in either open or closed grit patterns. On open grit papers the particles are spread farther apart to prevent "clogging" when doing coarse heavy sanding. Most coarse grit sanding discs are of the open grit variety. If clogged with dust (not gummy), all papers can be cleaned with a wire brush.

Sandpapers are available with a variety of types of abrasives. The old-fashioned type simply used granules of silica sand as the grit. These granules are relatively soft in comparison to other abrasive grits and the sandpaper dulls easily when sanding hard surfaces. This type would dull extremely fast if used to sand fiberglass, and consequently is not the best choice.

Three other types of abrasives are available: 1) Carborundum, which is black and usually found on "emery cloth"; 2) Aluminum oxide, which is brown, and is the most readily available; and 3) Silicon carbide, which is tan and also very good, but less available through retail outlets.

Sandpapers (the proper term is abrasive papers) are generally available in grits from 36 (very coarse) to 150 grit (relatively fine).

There are also "wet dry" papers which are available through most automotive supply houses and marine outlets. These papers are generally found in the finer and very fine grits ranging from 240 grit to 600 grit. They are constructed using a waterproof adhesive, so that they can be dipped in water and used wet. Using them wet prevents the fine sanding dust from clogging the very fine grit, as the water, which is used in liberal amounts, turns the dust into a slurry which does not clog the paper.

All sandpaper, when used, leaves scratch marks in the surface that has been sanded—the coarser the paper, the coarser and deeper the scratches.

Finishing with abrasive papers is chiefly a matter of simple common sense, once it is known what types of papers are available and basically how to use them.

If you must remove a lot of material, use a coarse grit paper. If you want to remove the scratches left from the coarse paper, continue by using a finer grit paper. By using successively finer papers to 150 grit, virtually all but the most minute scratches are removed until the surface feels smooth. This is generally sufficient for sanding wood, where a coat of paint or varnish will fill the minute scratches. On plastics, particularly polyesters, where no final coat of paint will be applied, the process must continue until the final surface is highly polished and mirror-smooth. After the 150 grit paper, a finer wet dry paper is used wet. You could start right off with a 600 grit paper, but this would be difficult and time consuming. After the 150 grit dry paper, lightly wet-sand the area with a medium wet dry paper such as 240 grit to remove the scratches left by the 150 grit. Follow this by wet-sanding with a 400 grit wet dry, and then a 600 grit wet dry. This will almost leave the surface polished with very little effort required for the following rubbing and polishing procedures. If 600 grit paper is not available, you could stop with 400 grit, but then it would take a little extra effort with the compounds.

Although the foregoing sounds like quite a few unnecessary steps, it produces the quickest results with the least effort.

Polishing Compounds

Like abrasive papers, there are many types of polishing compounds available. The most generally available are automotive types—such as Du Pont's # 7 Red Rubbing Compound or Du Pont's # 101S White Lacquer Rubbing Compound. Either one can be used alone to effect a final finish, but since the red is slightly coarser than the white, it is recommended that both be used. The red should be used first, followed by the white, if a lot of polishing is anticipated. This will save time and effort in the long run.

Methods of Sanding and Equipment Used

Hand Sanding: The most common type of sanding is simple hand sanding whereby the paper is folded and held between the thumb and fingers. This method is generally used for abrading and wet dry sanding. It is not used when "high spots" are to be removed, as the flexibility of the paper backed by the fingers will readily follow the contours in the surface and not remove the high spots alone.

For hand sanding, take a typical 9″ x 11″ piece of abrasive paper and cut it from side to side into three equal strips of approximately 9″ x 3½″. The cuts do not have to be precise. Take one of the cut pieces and fold it in three equal parts so that the result is a three-thickness pad of approximately 3″ x 3″. You will now have three separate surfaces with which to sand: the top, the bottom, and the one in the middle which can be unfolded and brought to the top. If you follow this procedure, you will get the most efficiency from your abrasive papers.

Block Sanding: This method is used to remove high spots without sanding the adjacent low spots. It is used to final featheredge gel coat repairs or to remove bumps from the finished work. Although there are block sanding devices available through most hardware stores which hold the paper by means of clips, in many instances they have soft padded surfaces. These padded surfaces allow the abrasive paper to slightly follow contours in the surface and are not suitable for removing high spots in the hard polyester. If a hand block is not available, a small block of wood is most suitable. In this instance, cut a block of wood large enough to accommodate the 1/3 strip of abrasive paper, and wrap the paper around it. The paper can be hand held on the block, or the ends fastened with thumbtacks or masking tape.

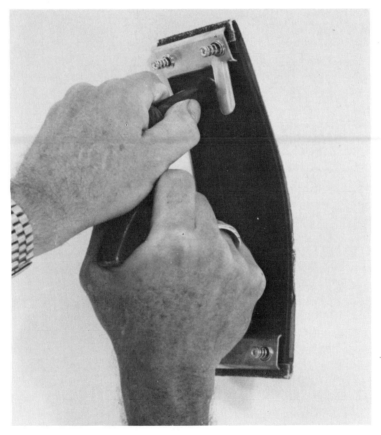

Flex Sander.

For the professional, there is available through automotive distributors, a hard but flexible plastic abrasive paper holder with a base plate of 3″ x 9¾″. Our particular one is known as a "Flex Sander." Although the backing is flexible, it is not padded, and has two handles similar to those on a wood plane. It also has clips to hold the abrasive paper. It is an excellent tool, particularly for trying to remove the high spots from a contoured surface as that found on a boat bow.

When removing high spots with a block sander, use medium paper such as 80 or 100 grit. The scratches are then removed by simple hand sanding using finer papers. Once all high spots are removed, hand sanding or sanding with a padded vibrator sander can continue.

Vibrator Sanders: Though not absolutely necessary for finishing work, vibrator sanders are very useful. They can be used for coarse, medium or fine sanding and are available in straightline and orbital, or combination, types. Either can be used, although the orbital or combination type is generally preferred. They always have a soft padded back-up pad, and consequently are not suitable for removing high spots. A thin piece of plywood or sheet metal can be inserted between the soft back-up pad and the back of the abrasive paper to make the vibrator sander useful for removing high spots. This stiffener should have an old piece of abrasive paper glued to the back side of it (the side that will go against the soft padded backing) to prevent it from sliding out from between the pad and the paper when sanding.

Vibrators can be used as they are for normal, medium and fine dry sanding once the high spots have been sanded smooth. For wet use, with wet dry papers, a piece of thin plastic should be used between the pad and the back of the wet dry paper to keep the soft pad from becoming saturated with water. The plastic should be cut about one inch wider than the paper to help keep water from getting in at the edges.

Disc Sanders: These are almost indispensable in making fiberglass boat repairs, as they are capable of removing large amounts of materials with a minimum of effort, using coarse open grit papers. They generally rotate at about 5,000 revolutions per minute and are not suitable for polishing operations requiring slower speeds.

In the event that a disc sander is not available, a ¼" electric drill with a rubber flexible sanding pad can be used. It will not be as fast, but will do the job, and if used with a variable-speed drill, even finishing operations with wet dry paper can be accomplished. Discs can be cut from wet dry paper and affixed to the rubber sanding pad, using very slow speeds and light pressures for wet-sanding. Lamb's wool bonnets can likewise be attached for subsequent polishing operations. When used properly, they become an invaluable tool for the professional as well as the amateur.

Polishers: Polishers should not exceed 2,500 revolutions per minute, as considerable friction and heat are developed when polishing with an abrasive compound. In this event, the heat could soften the polyester sufficiently to cause staining and discoloration. Lamb's wool or soft cloth pads should be used and thoroughly "wetted out" with the compound before polishing. Additional compound can be applied by hand to the surface to be polished, to assure a sufficient quantity of compound before commencing.

Polishing can also be accomplished entirely by hand. Compound is applied to a cloth pad, and the area is rubbed with vigorous pressure until the desired luster is achieved.

If after polishing is completed, scratches are noticed; the area should be wet sanded again and re-polished. Scratches indicate insufficient wet dry sanding before polishing.

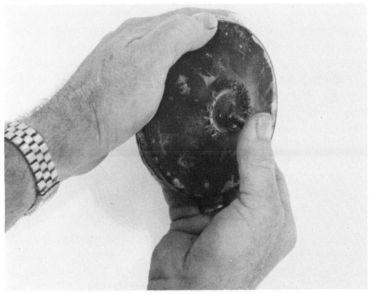

Close-up showing a swivel head rubber sanding disc for an electric drill. The stem is molded into the rubber pad and will flex from side to side; this minimizes edge-gouging. Washer-attached spindles are more rigid and have more of a tendency to cause edge-gouging.

Portable Hand-held Belt Sanders: These are generally useless in making boat repairs, as they are designed for sanding perfectly flat surfaces, such as boards. There are not many "perfectly flat" surfaces on a fiberglass boat. When used on surfaces having a slight curve or compound curve, they have a tendency to gouge on the edges when they are slightly tilted.

In conclusion, it should be pointed out that a very major portion of fiberglass boat repair involves sanding and polishing. Structural repairs are relatively easy, but the final finishing requires great patience. It is this portion of the repair that is exposed and is on display for all to see.

6.

CLEANUP PROCEDURES

Working with fiberglass and polyesters is a messy occupation. However, it can be made more bearable and less expensive by following a few simple rules.

First, wear old clothes. If catalyzed polyesters get on your clothes (they inevitably will) and they are not removed immediately while in the liquid state, they will cure as a part of your clothing. There is no known solvent for cured polyesters. In over two decades of working with polyesters, I have never managed to stay far enough away from the stuff to keep from ruining the clothes I was wearing.

Acetone is the most efficient cleaner and solvent for liquid polyesters. There are other less efficient solvents, including lacquer thinners, styrene, chlorothene, alcohol, and even hot water and detergent. Acetone is available through most marine outlets in small quantities. It is sold in large quantities (5 gal. and up) by most chemical distributors.

Acetone is a highly volatile material (having a flash point of $0°F$.). However, unlike many other solvents, the fumes are very light and dissipate almost immediately upon evaporation. When acetone burns, it burns very much like alcohol—with a clear blue smokeless flame. Acetone should always be used with adequate ventilation to prevent concentrations of fumes from building up to a combustible mixture. Acetone will dissolve rayon instantly, so rayon clothing should be avoided.

For brush cleaning: Keep acetone in three covered cans. Wipe the excess resin from the brush with a paper towel, and then clean the brush successively in each of the three cans. After many cleanings, the acetone in the first can will become thick with resin contamination. Discard this, fill the can with clean acetone and move it to the third position. By rotating the cans in this fashion, very little acetone will be wasted and brushes will last indefinitely. Keep the lids on the cans when they are not in use. The volatile acetone will evaporate completely in a few days if not kept covered.

Sanding fiberglass produces a dust which is laden with minute fiberglass filaments. This dust is very irritating to the skin and acts like an itching powder. It is best to wear long pants and long-sleeved shirts when sanding, as this reduces exposure and therefore discomfort. Protective cremes, such as Du Pont's Protex, can be applied to the exposed skin before sanding. Protective cremes are available at paint supply stores. When power sanding, a face mask or respirator is a good precaution.

Clothes worn while sanding should always be laundered separately. This will prevent contamination of the entire wash and resultant itching suffered by the entire family.

7.

REPAIRING SMALL GOUGES IN GEL COAT

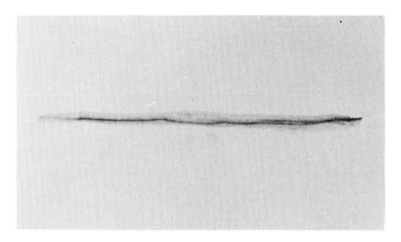

Small gouge in gel coat surface, less than 1/8″ deep with no serious structural damage.

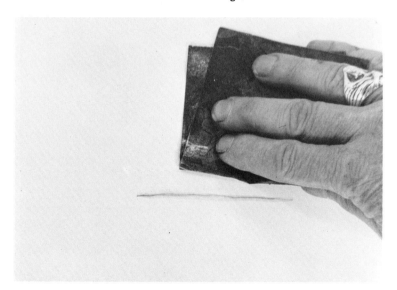

Using fine sandpaper (150 grit), lightly sand the scratch area and the area adjacent to it. This will assure a good bond to the existing gel coat surrounding the scratch. If desirable, a small abrasive burr or carbide burr can be used with a ¼″ electric drill to remove jagged edges.

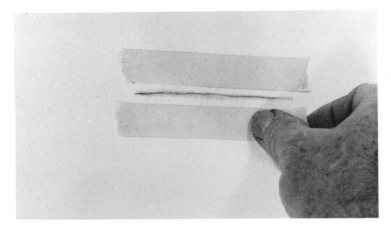

After sanding, wipe the surface clean and place a strip of masking tape along each edge at the scar, extending at least ½" beyond the ends. The 6 mil thickness of the masking tape will assure a build-up of sufficient thickness of the gel coat to be applied to allow it to be "featheredged."

If the scar is in an area that has a severe convex curve, more than one thickness of masking tape may be necessary to assure a buildup over the curved area.

Mix a small amount of gel coat with the proper amount of catalyst. It is best to use a board as a palette and disperse the catalyst into the gel coat with a putty knife. This assures more complete mixing when using very small amounts.

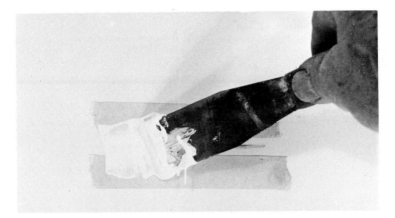

With a small putty knife apply the catalyzed gel coat in the area between the two strips of masking tape, filling the area to the thickness of the tape. Then apply an extra amount between the tapes at the end where you intend to start. Remove surplus materials from the tape and outside edges.

Take a piece of plastic wrap, 4" to 6" wide and hold or tape it at the beginning end. Hold the trailing end up away from the wet gel coat to keep from entrapping air. With a clean putty knife using light pressure on the upper surface of the plastic wrap, pull the "bead" of excess gel coat under the plastic film toward the opposite end with a slow steady stroke, letting the trailing edge of the plastic film contact the wet gel coat as the putty knife progresses. A piece of round dowel or pencil can be used instead of the putty knife, if you have trouble "snagging" the thin plastic film. Check thoroughly for entrapped air bubbles through the clear plastic. If they are present, rework or repeat the procedure if necessary. Considering that there is such a minute amount of material involved, several "test runs" can be made over any smooth surface until the technique is perfected.

Stretch the plastic wrap with the fingers and with small tabs of masking tape, adhere the stretched plastic wrap to the boat surface completely around the four edges of the wrap. This will assure a smooth wrinkle-free surface which will be easier to sand smooth after the gel coat has cured and hardened. After gel coat has hardened, peel the plastic wrap and masking tape from the area. The gel coat, even if air-inhibited, should cure to a hard tack-free surface because the plastic wrap will keep the air from the upper surface while it is curing.

Note: Some brands of plastic wrap will leave a slightly tacky upper surface on the cured polyester after they have been removed. If this does occur simply wipe the area with acetone to remove the tacky residue prior to sanding.

With a wood block and fine sandpaper (150 grit or finer), sand along the edges of the repair to featheredge it into the old surface, taking care not to cut into the old surrounding gel coat. This step can also be accomplished very quickly using a ¼″ drill with a rubber sanding pad using fine paper (250-400 grit) and using very light pressure. A variable speed drill is best as it allows speed control and very fine sanding.

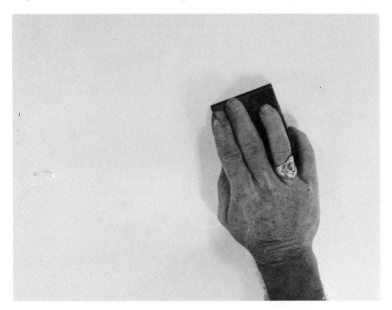

With 400 grit wet dry paper, using it with water, complete the featheredging and remove the light scratches left from the preceding sandpaper. If 600 grit wet dry paper is available, further polish the area with it, using it wet, to minimize effort and time with the polishing compound.

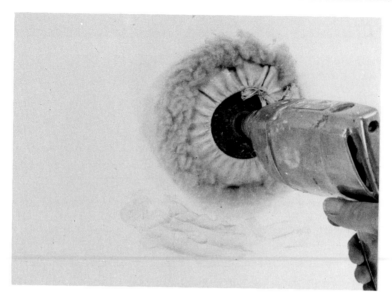

Apply the paste polishing compound to the area. Polish the area to a high gloss with a lamb's wool buffing wheel on a polisher or electric drill (not to exceed 2500 RPM). This can also be done by hand using a cloth pad and considerable pressure and "elbow grease." If scratches remain, repeat the process with the wet dry paper and polishing compound. Apply a coat of wax and polish as a final step.

8.

HOLE IN HULL OR OTHER STRUCTURAL AREAS

Crack or hole completely through the hull, when the inside of the hull is accessible. This will require both structural and cosmetic repairs and the finished repair should be stronger than the original hull.

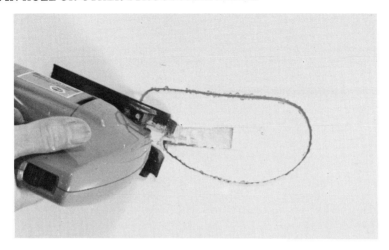

Using a saber saw with a metal cutting blade, remove damaged area making sure that no cracks or weak spots extend into the remaining area. Always cut the hole round, or with round corners, to relieve subsequent stress.

With an abrasive burr or carbide burr, featheredge the outside of the hole until a "knife" edge exists along the entire perimeter of the hole. A small disc sander may also be used for this operation.

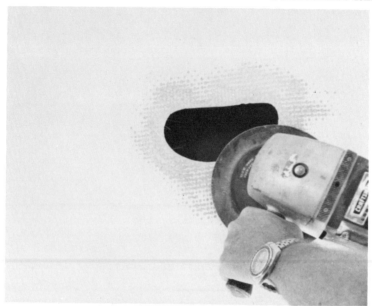

With a disc sander, grind away old surface to present clean fiberglass
to at least 3″ from the edges of the hole on the inside of the hull.
Featheredge the edges tapering them toward the outer surfaces.

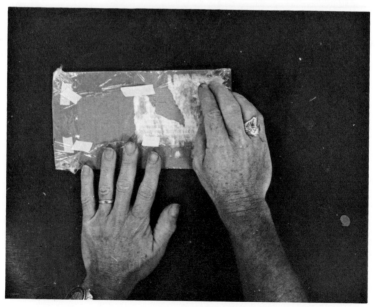

Cut a piece of stiff cardboard or corrugated board at least 2″ (all
around) larger than the hole area. Cover it with plastic wrap, taping
the edges of the wrap to the back side.

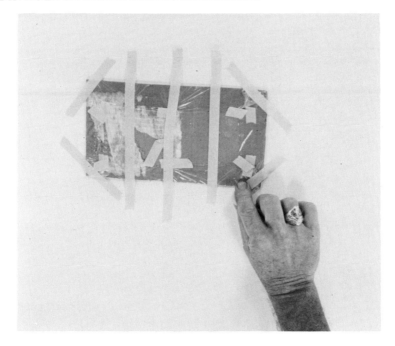

Take the plastic wrapped cardboard and securely tape it with masking tape over the hole on the outside of the hull.

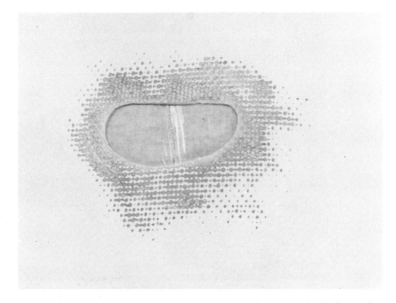

This shows the cardboard taped to the outside of the hull, from the inside. The plastic wrapped cardboard will be the surface which you will work against, so it should be very securely taped to the outside.

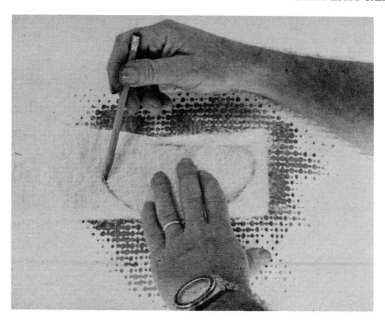

Mark and cut pieces of fiberglass matt and cloth or roving to fit
inside of the hole. Sufficient pieces should be cut so that, when
wetted out with resin, they will fill the hole.

Using clear laminating resin, apply a coat of resin to the plastic wrap
covering the hole, and then place the precut piece of matt into the wet
resin. Wet this matt out and continue building up with alternate plies
of matt, cloth, or roving, matt, etc., wetting out each ply individually.

After the hole is filled, take larger pieces of matt and cloth or roving and build up over the patch area to at least the hull thickness. These patches should overlap the hole edges by at least 2 to 3 inches.

After the inner patch has cured, remove the cardboard/plastic wrap and featheredge the outside laminate which was against the plastic wrap to assure a bond.

Apply precut layers of matt, or matt, cloth and matt to the feather-edged area and wet out with laminating resin. Build this patch up to a thickness higher than the adjacent area.

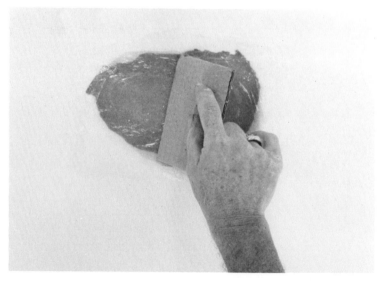

Cover the area with a piece of plastic wrap and, using a squeegee or a piece of stiff cardboard as a squeegee, squeegee out all air bubbles, working from the center toward the edges.

Stretch the plastic wrap tightly over the wet patch by pulling and taping the edges with masking tape. Using the squeegee, smooth out the patch to remove all "waves" or high spots.

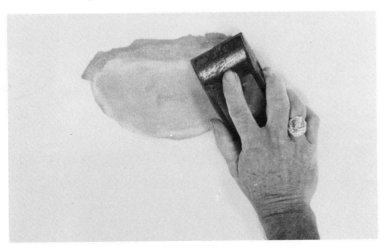

After the outer patch has cured, remove the plastic wrap and sand the area smooth with a block and medium sandpaper (150 grit). This can also be done with a disc sander using light pressure so as not to gouge the surface.

Dust the surface and apply two coats of surfacing gel coat, allowing
the first coat to cure and lightly sanding between coats.

After the final coat of surfacer gel coat has cured, lightly sand the
area, featheredging to the surrounding area using fine abrasive paper
(about 240 grit). This can be done with a hand block or with a
swivel hand disc sander on an electric drill, using slow speed and very
light pressure.

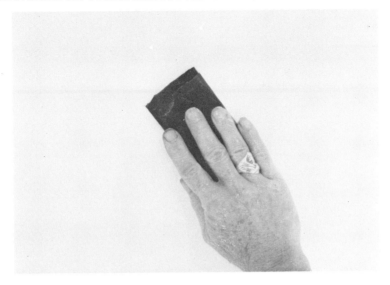

Wet dry sand the area using 400 grit followed by 600 grit paper, using them wet, to remove all scratches. If you sand through an area, letting the fiberglass show through, dry the surface and repeat the gel coat and sanding process.

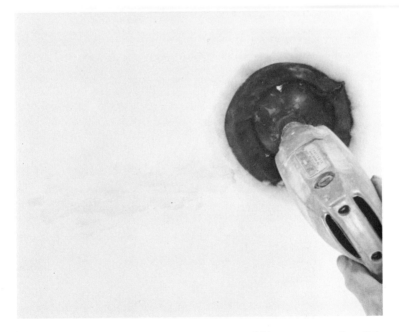

Using a lamb's wool pad and polishing or rubbing compound, polish the area. This can also be done by hand, using a cloth pad and considerable "elbow grease."

9.

REPAIRING HOLE IN HULL OR OTHER STRUCTURAL AREAS WHERE INSIDE IS INACCESSIBLE

To repair a hole in the hull where the inside of the hull is inaccessible, cut out the damaged area with a saber saw as described in the previous sequence. Featheredge the hole to a "knife edge" from the outside, using a disc sander.

Take a piece of coarse sandpaper and thoroughly sand the inside of the hull area to a distance of 3″ or 4″ from the hole edge. This will have to be accomplished by reaching inside the hole from the outside.

Cut a piece of stiff heavy corrugated board 3″ larger all around than the hole size. Place the cardboard on a flat working surface and apply precut pieces of matt and woven cloth or roving in alternate layers, beginning with matt and ending with matt. Each ply of reinforcement should be layed up and wet out separately using catalyzed lay-up or laminating resin. All air bubbles should be removed using the brush bristle ends in a "tamping" action. Build up laminate to at least twice the hull thickness.

Thoroughly apply a liberal coat of resin to the uppermost ply of matt, as this coat will have to be of sufficient thickness to squeeze out and effect the bond of the laminate to the inside of the hull surface.

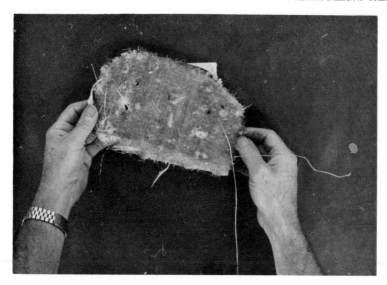

Punch holes through the back side of the cardboard and through the laminate so that thin stiff wire loops can be inserted from the back and left extended out the front through the wetted out fiberglass. This should, of course, be done while the laminate is still wet. Holes should be punched in pairs to accommodate as many wire loops as required.

Take the wet laminate on the cardboard backing and carefully slip it through the cut-out hole, leaving the ends of the wires extending through to the outside. When slipping it through the hole, the wires will allow you to hold onto the piece without its falling, while you maneuver the piece sideways through the hole.

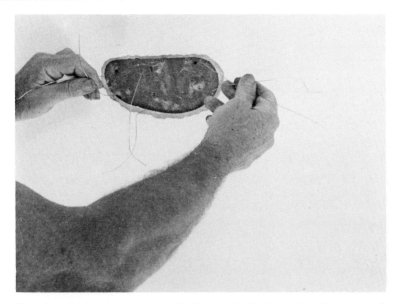

Position the laminate on the inside of the hole so that the edges of the laminate have a 3″ overlap on the inside of the hull. Pull the wires toward you to temporarily hold the laminate in position.

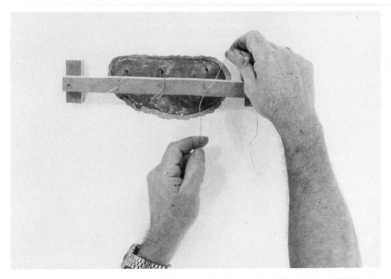

Cut a piece of stick longer than the hole, and nail two small blocks of wood to the ends to hold the stick away from the hull. (This should actually be done before preparing the laminate and putting it into position.) Let the stick straddle the pair of extended wire ends so that each pair of wires can be pulled and twisted around the stick to hold the laminate firmly in place. If desirable, small strips of masking tape can be used to hold the stick in place while working.

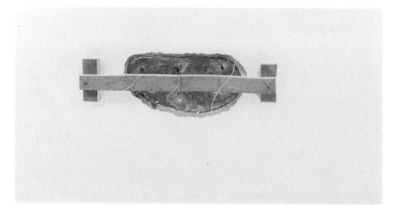

After the laminate is in place, held by the stick and twisted wires, double check to assure that the wet laminate is pressed firmly against the inside of the hull surface and the surplus lay-up resin is squeezed out. If necessary, loosen one pair of wires at a time and pull tighter and retwist. Allow the laminate to cure.

When the laminate has cured, untwist the wires and remove the wood brace. Use a pair of wire cutters to snip the wires off even with the laminate. Using a disc sander, featheredge the outside surface to the interior patch and proceed to repair the exterior in accordance with the procedures described previously in the sequence on repairing holes through the hull.

10.

CRACKS OR HOLES OVER FLOTATION

Cut out ruptured fiberglass with grinder or saber saw. If possible, tilt the boat so that the hole is at the lowest part. This will allow drainage of the water which has saturated the foam flotation. Cut away the foam from the interior of the hull to at least 4″ from edge of hole. After water has drained and the remaining foam is completely dry, make repair as per sequence showing repair to hole in hull where interior is inaccessible.

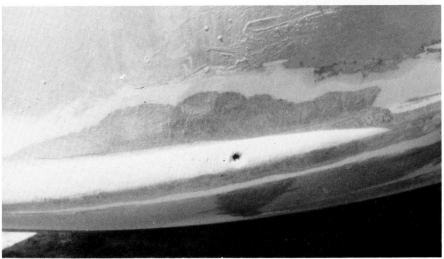

Cracks or holes over flotation.

11.

REPAIRING LARGE GOUGES (OVER 1/8″)

To effect a repair of this nature, it will be necessary to fill the crack area (if it is 1/8″ deep) with a fiberglass/polyester mixture before proceeding with the cosmetic repair.

Following are the steps which should be followed:

1. With an electric drill and an abrasive or carbide burr, clean out all loose or shattered material down to solid fiberglass. Widen the area if necessary. On each end of the crack enlarge the width of the gouge to produce a rounded area, which will relieve subsequent end strain.

2. Sand the area next to the gouge with fine sandpaper (150 grit).

3. Prepare a putty of fiberglass and gel coat. Some marine stores sell small packets of chopped or milled fiberglass strands for this purpose. If this is not available, your own chopped glass can be made in the following manner: With a pair of scissors, cut 1/8″ strips of glass matt and rub these strips between the palms of the hands until they fall apart into small chopped strands.

Catalyze the amount of gel coat necessary and mix the chopped glass with it to form a thick putty. Then *without* strips of masking tape along edges, apply this prepared putty into the void area with a putty knife. If the gouge is wider than ¼″, small narrow strips of fiberglass cloth or matt can be laminated inside the void area, instead of using a putty. To follow this procedure, a small amount of catalyzed gel coat or lay-up resin is applied into the void area with a small brush. Then apply successive strips of fiberglass, wetting out each one with resin until the void area is built up to a point slightly higher than the adjacent area.

After the void area has been filled, wipe off any excess resin from along the sides with acetone and a cloth. Place a piece of plastic wrap over the repaired area and smooth out and remove all air bubbles with a clean dry putty knife.

Then, to remove all wrinkles, use small tabs of masking tape, stretch the plastic wrap and tape the edges in a similar manner as described in the previous sequence. Allow the repair to cure.

4. After curing, remove the plastic wrap and sand the repair smooth so that it is even with, or slightly below, the adjacent areas. This can be done with a block of wood and sandpaper, or carefully with a small rubber disc sander on a ¼″ electric drill.

5. Remove all dust and apply two strips of masking tape, as described in the previous sequence, along the edges of the repair.

6. After this, follow the steps described in the previous sequence: Mix gel coat; apply gel coat between the strips of masking tape; apply the plastic wrap and remove wrinkles and air bubbles with a putty knife; tape the edges of the plastic wrap to stretch it tight; allow to cure; block sand; wet dry sand; buff and polish; and give final waxing.

If it is suspected that the gouge has structurally weakened the hull, then a further structural repair must be made on the inside of the hull surface. This type of repair will be described in detail in the following chapter.

12.

CRACKS THROUGH HULL OR DECK

If the crack is over an area where the inside is inaccessible, a hole will have to be cut with a saber saw, and the repair made in accordance with preceeding chapter, describing holes in the hull where the inside is inaccessible.

If you can get at the inside, the repair is much easier. Clean all grease and dirt from the inside portion with a strong detergent and water solution. Thoroughly sand the inside area with coarse paper, either by hand or with a disc grinder.

Photo showing repositioning of sprung, ruptured deck. A 2 x 4 with plastic wrap on the bottom is clamped to realign sprung sections prior to repair.

Then determine whether the two edges are "sprung" and do not meet evenly. If they are sprung, the two edges should be repositioned, so that they match up on an even plane before the repair is started. This can be accomplished with a board and "C" clamps fastened to the outside surface. The board should be covered with plastic wrap or wax paper to prevent resin from sticking to it. Small wedges may be necessary to true up the edge after the board is in place. If the crack is in an area where "C" clamps cannot be used, then it will be necessary to drill small holes through the hull and attach the board on the outside by using wood screws from the inside.

Once the two edges are mated, ¼″ holes should be drilled at each end of the crack to relieve subsequent stress.

If "C" clamps were used, apply several layers of matt and woven cloth or roving wetted out with catalyzed resin over the crack area on the inside of the hull, extending at least 3″ on each side and each end of the crack.

If screws were used, it will be necessary to make temporary patches between the screw heads on the inside to hold the edges in place. To do this, use matt and cloth or roving in between the exposed screw heads being careful not to laminate over the screw heads. Small strips of masking tape can be used over the screw heads to keep the liquid resin from attaching them permanently. Once the temporary patches have cured, remove the screws and stiffening board and proceed to laminate the entire area over the screw holes as well with matt and woven cloth or roving as previously described. If a tack-free resin was used to make the temporary patches, they will have to be lightly sanded to assure a bond between them and the final inside patch.

After the inside patch has cured, use an abrasive or carbide burr to remove all fractured material down to the inside patch. When this is completed, follow the procedure previously described for repairing deep gouges.

Once the inside reinforcement is accomplished, the outside repair can be tackled. Grind away all loose or fractured material with a burr grinder to assure only solid fiberglass is left. After this, proceed to repair the outside and gel coat as previously described for repairing large gouges over 1/8″.

13.

BLISTERS OR AIR HOLES BETWEEN GEL COAT
AND FIRST LAMINATE

This condition is caused by faulty workmanship. Although there is no serious structural impairment involved, such areas should be repaired to prevent the exposed fiberglass fibers from wicking water and gradually eroding.

With a knife, chip away all the edges of the gel coat that are not firmly bonded to the laminate. Tap adjacent areas with a coin. If a hollow sound reveals more blisters, chip them away also.

Bevel the edges of the holes with a Carborundum or carbide burr grinder. Sand about one inch beyond the edges with fine sandpaper to assure a bond for the final surface coat.

If the hole is small and less than ¼'' wide, fill it with polyester putty (auto body patching compound). If the hole is larger, fill it with a mixture of chopped glass and gel coat as previously described.

Allow the patch to cure and sand smooth with a block sander.

Brush on a surfacing gel coat. Sand, wet dry, and polish. If the defect is on a flat area, which seldom is the case, the final steps can be completed with the plastic wrap technique instead of sanding.

14.

RECOATING LARGE AREAS
WITH A POLYESTER SURFACE COAT

This is a major undertaking, but can be done by anyone willing to expend the time and effort. Even though the epoxy paints are easy to apply, they will chalk in a few years and lose their luster. This does not happen to properly applied polyesters and, consequently, some boat owners will have nothing else but a polyester coating. The major disadvantage of polyester coatings is that they cannot be applied in a perfect "self leveling" coating, and must be mechanically finished (sanded, wet dried, and polished) if a factory mold finish is to be expected.

Sand the entire surface to be coated with fine sandpaper (about 150 grit). This can be done by hand, with a vibrator pad sander or with a soft disc sander using a flexible swivel head. A firm rubber disc sander is unsuitable, as it would leave gouges which would be hard to cover up. If cracks or gouges are present, they should first be repaired according to previous instructions. When final sanding is complete, the surface should be free of flaws and perfectly smooth. *Do not* touch the sanded surface with the bare hands as this will leave traces of skin oil on the surface and cause the subsequent polyester surface coating to "crawl."

Once sanded, wipe the entire surface with acetone and a clean cloth. After the acetone has evaporated, rewipe the surface using a clean "tac" cloth (available through automotive supply houses) to remove all traces of dust.

Mask off all adjacent areas rubbing the masking tape very firmly with the fingertip covered with cloth, to assure no "weeping" under the edge of the tape.

The actual coating can be done by brush or spray, but spray equipment necessary to spray the high viscosity polyesters is very expensive and generally only used by the larger industrial or commercial users. Spraying a uniform coat of polyester, even with the expensive industrial equipment, also requires a very skilled operator. Brushing is the most logical choice in most cases.

Choose a good pure bristle brush with tapered bristle ends. Avoid brushes which are either too stiff or too soft. For most work, a 3″ or 4″ wide brush will suffice, and if there is considerable "trim," a narrow trim brush should also be on hand.

Do not work in the direct sunlight. Choose a shady location or an overcast day.

Dust and flying insects have an affinity for wet polyesters, so, if possible, pick a time of day or location where they are minimal.

Check your material for pot life and thixotropy (vertical holding power). The material should have surfacing additive added—or converted to a surfacing resin as previously described. It should be heavy enough so that it can be "flowed" on with the brush in a heavy (10 mil) coating without draining. Regular gel coats are generally thixotropic enough, but if they are too thick, they can be thinned with a small amount of styrene which is a non-evaporative thinner for polyesters. If styrene is not available, small amounts of lay-up resin can be added.

You should catalyze your material so that it cures as quickly as possible within your working time. Generally one-quart batches are mixed at a time, and this amount can easily be brushed in 20 minutes.

Stir in the catalyst thoroughly for at least one minute. Wipe the sides and bottom with the stirring stick to assure that there is no uncatalyzed resin clinging to the sides of the container. In fact, it is a good practice to pour the mixed polyester from the mixing container into another container used for application. This further assures that no uncatalyzed material is clinging to the sides.

"Lay on" the material in a heavy thickness using horizontal strokes, working from top to bottom. Avoid rebrushing as this could remove the waxy surface additive film. Always lap while wet, as polyesters do not lose solvents as paints do.

Make sure that you clean your brushes in acetone after each quart is applied, and thoroughly shake and dry the brushes to assure that no acetone is left in the brush (or metal frame holding the bristles) before using again.

Generally one heavy coat is sufficient. However, if you have opacity problems, two coats may be necessary with a light sanding between coats.

There are other commercial materials and techniques used to apply surface coats, but the materials and equipment involved are not readily available to the average craftsman.

Once the coating has cured, it should then be block-sanded using a fine paper (about 240 grit) to remove all brush marks and high spots. Following this, it should be wet-sanded with 400 grit, then 600 grit wet dry sandpaper, and polished and waxed.

With this technique you can duplicate a factory finish gel coat, but with considerable work, as previously stated. In the final analysis, the results are well worth the effort.

15.

DETERIORATED GEL COAT

This disintegrated condition is caused by a faulty gel coat or a faulty application of the gel coat. It does not show up for several years.

The only solution is to sand away the eroded gel coat down to the fiberglass and apply a new surface coat. Do not attempt just a light surface sanding. If all of the eroded gel coat is not removed and re-placed, the new surface coat will develop cracks corresponding to the old cracks underneath.

Once the surface has been sanded, do not touch or rub it with the fingers. This leaves a slight oily residue and will cause the coating to crawl. Brush on a surfacing gel coat. The new gel coat should be fairly thick and overlap the sanded edges. Do not apply a surfacing resin gel coat in hot sun; this melts the waxy additive.

After the new gel coat has cured, proceed with hand block sanding, wet dry sanding, and polishing.

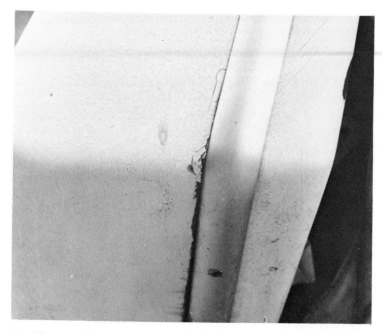

Severely eroded gel coat: This was due to the manufacturer's use of acetone as a thinner for the gel coat. This surface is over ten years old, and did not show signs of deterioration until the boat was four years old. Once started, the deterioration gets progressively worse each year. There is no structural damage involved, but for cosmetic purposes the entire area will have to be sanded down to glass reinforcement and be coated.

16.

STAR CRACKS OR SPIDER WEB CRACKS
IN GEL COAT

This condition is caused when the gel coat is too thick, or too brittle, or when the laminate beneath it is too thin and therefore stresses excessively.

These areas must be sanded down to the fiberglass base. If they are only lightly sanded and recoated, the cracks will reappear through the new coat.

If there are only a few isolated cracks, grind them down with an abrasive burr or a carbide burr. Then lightly sand the entire area, and proceed as if you were repairing a gouge.

If there are numerous cracks close together, the entire area should be sanded down to the fiberglass base.

The plastic wrap method of applying the gel coat can be used in some sites. If the area is too wide for this, then a coat of surfacing gel coat should be brushed on. Sand and polish as previously described.

"Star Crack" or "Spider Web Cracks" through Gel Coat: In this instance, the cracks were caused by the laminate being too thin for its intended use. They were caused by the stress put on the laminate by the stanchion mounting brackets.

This area started showing cracks when the boat was two years old, and the owner lightly sanded the area and applied another coat of surfacer gel coat. Within a year, the cracks reappeared through the new gel coat corresponding to the location of the old cracks.

17.

LIGHT SCRATCHES AND SCUFF MARKS

Light scratches, scuff marks, and stains are not serious because they do not structurally weaken the hull. Many boat owners simply ignore them. When they can be easily corrected, it is worthwhile to do so.

You will need 600 grit wet dry sandpaper and polishing or rubbing compound. Using the 600 paper wet, very carefully try one small area. If the gel coat is sufficiently thick and the scratches are quite light, you will be able to remove them with the 600 paper without sanding through the existing gel coat. A final polishing will restore the finish to its original appearance.

Deeper scratches should be filled with a matching gel coat before sanding. Lightly sand the area surrounding the scratch, and catalyze a small amount of gel coat. Apply it to the scratch with a toothpick or small artist's brush. Cover the wet area with plastic wrap and stretch and tape the edges as previously described. It is not necessary to use strips of masking tape along the sides of the scratch if it is not actually a gouge. Wet-sand the cured gel coat with the 600 grit paper on a block to remove high spots, then wet dry sand by hand to feather the edges. Follow this by buffing, polishing, and waxing.

18.

GLITTER FINISHES

Glitter-finished gel coats have become extremely popular with the younger set as they are unique in appearance and have great sales appeal. To repair such a finish is most unappealing for it involves a tedious procedure.

First, let us consider how they are produced, as this will help in understanding how to repair them. The manufacturer first applies a clear gel coat to his polished mold and lets it gel. Then he blows the particles of metallic or plastic glitter into the tacky gel coat. Following this, he sprays on another coat of clear gel coat and lets it gel, after which he sprays on a coat of pigmented back-up coat, which is actually the background color. Then, of course, he continues with his fiberglass lay-up. When the piece is popped out of the mold, the visual appearance is backwards from the sequence of application. On the exterior surface you now see the clear gel coats with the glitter particles suspended between them, backed up by the opaque pigmented back-up color coat.

To repair such a finish, you must work backwards from the manufacturer's original procedure; you have no mold to work against and instead of producing your finish from the outside in, you will make your repair from the inside out.

First, you will need a matching background color. In many instances, the boat manufacturer can supply this in small quantities. The same applies to the particles of glitter. Considering that this is the only practical course, every effort should be made to locate the manufacturer and supply him with the information he will need to send you the color and glitter.

If the manufacturer is no longer in business, or if the materials are unavailable, your chances of coming up with an identical color match are very slim. Under these circumstances, the best you can hope for is to locate "close" pigments at a marine supply outlet and intermix them to match the color as closely as possible. I know of an instance where colored chalk was purchased, shaved into a powder and mixed with clear resin to produce the desired shade. This technique will work, but requires infinite patience and many tests.

If glitter is not available through the boat manufacturer, try the various hobby shops, sign supply houses, or art shops.

Next, make whatever structural repairs are necessary in accordance with the previous chapters, eliminating the steps involving the gel coat. Before proceeding with the cosmetic portion of your repair, it would be best to make a sample on a small piece of wood or stiff cardboard to test your proficiency and color match.

Catalyze a small amount of air-inhibited resin with the pigment added and apply it to the piece of wood. If you only have non-air-inhibited resin (tack-free), it will be necessary to let it cure and sand the surface before proceeding. Sanding scratches will cause a dark colored resin to turn light, but as soon as a clear resin is applied to the surface, the scratches will disappear and the original color will reappear.

Following this, apply a coat of clear resin and blow the glitter particles into the wet clear resin. This can be accomplished by shaking the glitter from a salt shaker or perforated can. Another technique is to use a "rose duster" such as can be purchased from garden supply shops. Care should be taken to apply only as much glitter as is in the original finish; too much glitter concentrated in an area will stick out like the proverbial sore thumb.

The resin used in this application should be air-inhibited (tacky) to allow a bond to exist between it and the final coat of clear. With the glitter suspended in the surface of this coat of resin, it would be impossible to sand between coats; so if you only had non-air-inhibited resin, you will have to assure that it will cure with a tacky surface. You can do this by applying external heat as described in Chapter 2, on "Non-air-inhibited resins." This heat, which can be provided by a heat lamp, hair dryer, or hot air blower, will melt the paraffin additive in the liquid resin and cause it to cure with a tacky surface. Apply the source of heat as soon as the glitter has been applied into the wet resin, and keep it on until the resin has gelled or cured. This same technique can be used on the previously applied pigmented background color coat if desired.

If heat was used, allow the area to cool and then apply the final coat of non-air-inhibited clear resin. After this coat has cured, proceed with sanding, buffing, and polishing in order to check the final product.

If you are not satisfied, make whatever modifications you deem necessary on another small sample.

Once you are satisfied with the results, repeat the operation over the repaired area on the actual boat surface.

Testing before making the actual repair is always recommended, because pigmented polyesters always take on a slightly different shade from the liquid state to the cured state. The two clear top coats also influence the background color; this will have to be taken into account when matching the final color.

As you can see, repairing a glitter finish can be quite frustrating; in some instances so frustrating that the less experienced end up occasionally by making a simple structural repair and covering it with a pressure-sensitive decal.

19.

REPAIRING WEAK STRUCTURAL AREAS

If an area such as a hull is too weak and needs both stiffening and reinforcement for additional strength, the application of additional plies of fiberglass reinforcement is in order. This is always accomplished from the inside if possible. Doing it on the outside of a hull or deck top would require very extensive finishing (sanding and polishing) and would never be done unless absolutely unavoidable.

First, the area to be laminated must be scrubbed thoroughly with a scrub brush using a strong detergent and water to remove all traces of dirt, scum and grease or oil. After rinsing and drying, a thorough sanding with a disc grinder using medium to coarse paper on a flexible rubber disc backing would be necessary. Matt and woven roving should be cut and trimmed to cover the area involved and set aside. Both matt or woven roving can be cut and pieced (overlapped) in as many places as necessary, if one large piece is impractical. Woven roving is preferred over woven boat cloth for this purpose, as it builds up a much heavier laminate in one application and consequently is much more economical to use than boat cloth for the same thickness.

Next, catalyze the lay-up resin (air-inhibited) and apply it to the surface to be laminated and built up. Immediately apply the matt into the wet resin, and with more resin (using a brush or roller, or both) thoroughly saturate the matt from the top side. While this is still wet, apply the precut woven roving and saturate with more lay-up resin. If more than this one double laminate is required, the additional matt, roving, and resin can be applied at any time—wet on wet, or after the first composite laminate has gelled or cured.

After all of the fiberglass and lay-up resin has been applied and gelled or cured, a coat of surfacing resin (non-air-inhibited resin), either clear or pigmented, should be applied. An excellent formula for this final coat is a "flat" (non-glossy) pigmented finish which is not normally available to the small purchaser but which can be made by him on the spot. It not only produces a flat finish, but its "whipped-cream" consistency has excellent void-filling characteristics when brushed. It can be made in several ways. If you have access to floured fillers, such as floured talc or floured pumice, mix sufficient quantities of this material with surfacing resin (tack-free) to turn it into a whipped-cream consistency. Add pigment to give it opacity. This material can be hand-stirred in, or an electric drill with a small paint agitator can be used.

Another method is to mix a sufficient amount of paste filler, polyester putty or auto body patching compound in the same manner to the same consistency with the pigmented surfacing resin.

In both cases, check the pot life and cure time in a small amount to determine what the pot life and cure time will be. Some fillers may have a retarding effect on curing, while others may have an accelerating effect. Checking out a small sample and adjusting your catalyst ratio accordingly will assure predictable results.

Catalyze and apply this "flat" surfacer with a wide brush in a liberal application to fill all voids and render a smoother finish.

20.

ADDING STIFFENING TO WEAK
OR FLEXIBLE AREAS

Some areas, particularly small outboard decks, and sometimes hull areas where the contour is relatively flat with not much compound curve, the area will flex or "oilcan" under load. If it is not practical or economical to add another double ply of reinforcement to the entire area, stiffening "ribs" can be laminated in critical areas to add rigidity without great cost or weight. To do this, it is necessary to make a half tube or corrugated rib. This can be made from a cardboard mailing tube cut lengthwise, regular or balsa wood, or a strip of stiff polyurethane foam insulation. (Do not use styrofoam, as polyesters will dissolve it. If in doubt, check a small area with polyester. If it is styrofoam, it will dissolve, if polyurethane, it will not).

The half tube can have a radius of from ½″ to 2″ depending upon the amount of stiffness required. Once the laminate is completed and cured over the half tube, the laminate (not the half tube form) does the stiffening and gives the strength and support. Therefore, even cardboard serves well for this purpose, as it only provides the initial shape.

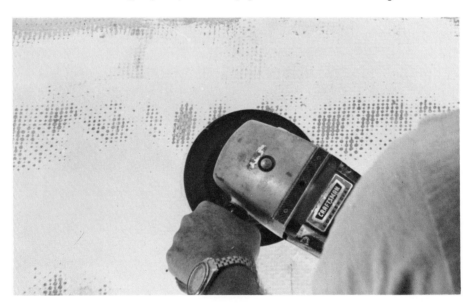

To stiffen a weak area with the "half tube" method, sand the interior surface with a disc grinder using coarse paper to assure a bond.

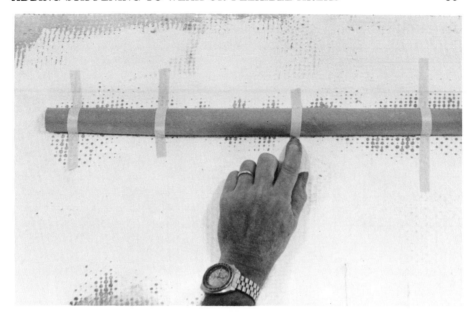

As the stiffening form, use a piece of cardboard mailing tube, cut in half lengthwise. A piece of half round wood or stiff polyurethane foam (not the foam rubber type), cut and formed into a half round shape, can also be used. Do not use styrofoam, as the polyester will melt it causing a soggy mess.

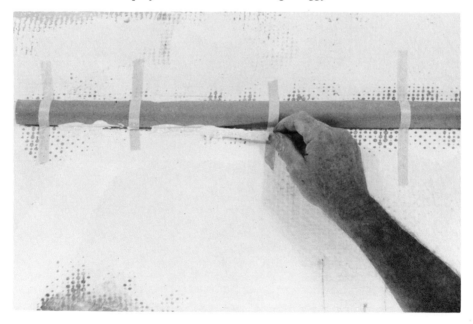

Use a catalyzed gel coat, putty or thickened lay-up resin as an intermediate adhesive. Apply it between the strips of masking tape with a "popsicle stick."

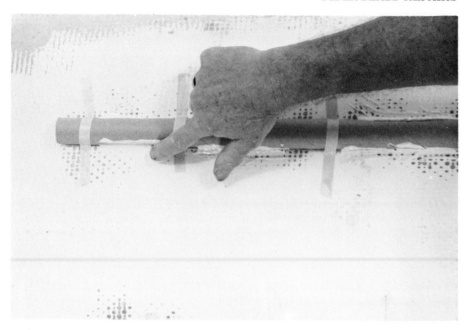

Smooth the applied adhesive with the fingertip in between the strips of masking tape to hold the half tube in place and to remove all ridges or uneven spots. After curing, remove the masking tape.

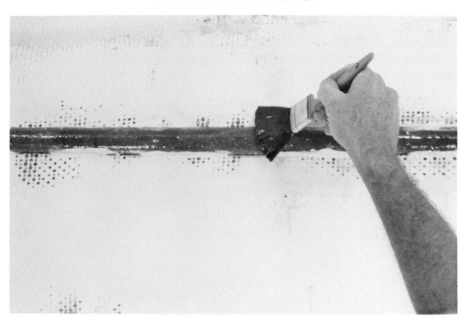

Brush a liberal coat of catalyzed clear laminating resin to the tube and at least two inches along each edge.

Apply precut strips of fiberglass matt into the wet resin and saturate it with more resin.

Apply alternate plies of roving or cloth and matt to build it up to the desired thickness (usually two plies of each are sufficient). After curing, smooth the rough edges by sanding, and the stiffening is complete. This "corrugated" effect will greatly stiffen a weak or flexible area without adding appreciable weight.

21.

GENERAL CARE AND MAINTENANCE
OF FIBERGLASS BOATS AND OTHER UNITS

Of all the materials used for boat construction, fiberglass boat surfaces are the easiest surfaces to maintain. To keep your boat in tiptop shape, it should be cleaned once or twice a year with a household or marine fiberglass detergent, followed by rinsing and waxing. Normal surface dirt will be removed with the detergent and you need not be afraid of using high concentrations of detergents or full-strength detergent.

Extremely stubborn stains of tar, grease, etc., can be removed with gasoline or lighter fluid if the detergent is ineffective.

Rust stains caused from ferrous metal can be removed by commercial rust removers or oxalic acid.

Stains which would not succumb to any of the foregoing methods will have to be removed with an abrasive cleaner, such as household scouring powders or 600 grit paper. When this is done, the cleaned surface will appear slightly dull and should be polished, as per Chapter 5, on sanding and polishing. If possible, remove a stain by chemical rather than abrasive means. If abrasives are used, buffing and polishing will be required to restore the luster.

Waxing: After cleaning, the surfaces should always be waxed, as this is the greatest deterrent to dirt, stains, and deterioration. Again, there are many automotive waxes which will do a good job. There are also many good marine waxes specifically for fiberglass boats.

If your gel coat has a chalky or dull appearance due to aging or lack of maintenance, it is generally a simple matter to restore it to its original luster and gloss by buffing, polishing, and waxing as previously mentioned.

Nicks, scratches, light gouges, or spider web cracks do not generally affect the strength of the boat, and when they are repaired, it is strictly for cosmetic purposes.

22.

THERMOPLASTIC BOATS

This book is written strictly about fiberglass/polyester boats. None of the information applies to the thermoformed plastic boats which have recently appeared—particularly in the canoe and dinghy trade. These boats are sometimes made from thermoplastics and cannot be repaired by the same techniques.

Thermoplastics readily soften or melt with the application of heat, therefore, if you touch a questionable surface with a hot object (such as the tip of a soldering iron), the material will melt immediately. This will not happen to thermosetting resins such as polyesters. If the material melts, it is not polyester/fiberglass and cannot be repaired by the techniques outlined in this book. Even though polyesters may soften slightly with the application of high heat, they cannot be melted such as thermoplastics.

If you are in doubt about the material in your boat, check with your dealer or manufacturer before proceeding.

23.

BUYING A FIBERGLASS BOAT

Never before has the old saying "Let the buyer beware" been more applicable to a given trade. Never before has the boat buyer been so at the mercy of the manufacturer. Inasmuch as the variety and combinations of reinforcements are many, the rule of common sense and experience should prevail.

1. *Check for hull thickness.* Insist that a through-hull fitting be removed to check the thickness of the hull. In general, the underwater portion of the hull should be at least double the thickness of the hull sides. Typical small boats of the 14- to 18-foot class should have a hull thickness of ¼″ to 5/16″ thickness on the underwater portion and 3/16″ to ¼″ on the upper hull. This thickness should increase progressively on the larger boats where their underwater section should be at least 5/8″ thick for a hull. Exceptions to this would be whaler type boats made under pressure-molding techniques. These boats generally have a higher glass content than conventional hand lay-up boats and are usually stiffened with a poured-in-place flotation foam sandwiched between an inner and outer shell.

2. *Check for stiffness.* If a hull flexes readily by pressure of the knee or hand, it can be assumed that this boat will "work" considerably more when involved with pounding waves. Such flexing generally indicates that the hull is too thin or does not have sufficient stiffness or compound curves to rigidify the hull sufficiently.

3. *Check for air bubbles.* These can be found by tapping the hull with a ring or coin, particularly along outside and inside corners, such as the transom or chine. Air bubbles, whether readily visible or found by tapping, indicate sloppy workmanship and inexperience.

4. *Check for fiberglass weave pattern in the exterior gel coat.* Although this condition does not weaken the boat, it does indicate inferior manufacturing procedures and should be avoided.

5. *Avoid red and blue colors if possible.* Some boat manufacturers do not use the most expensive pigments in their gel coats, particularly in certain colors. White, green, yellow and black pigments are generally inorganic and have very good nonfading characteristics. Blue and red, although available in inorganics, are very expensive, so the typical gel coat manufacturer uses organic reds and blues for cost reasons. These organic pigments generally fade in short order leaving the boat owner with additional maintenance. The same holds true for the "aqua" tones of green.

6. *Check for repaired areas.* These can be seen (and sometimes felt) upon close examination. Repaired areas indicate that the boat was either damaged or had a defective gel coat application. These do not necessarily indicate that the hull is weak, but do point to bad handling or manufacturing procedures.

7. *Check fastenings.* Screws or nuts and bolts should have washers. Cupped washers are recommended under the heads, and flat washers under the nuts. Fastenings not properly washered will have a tendency to pull through the fiberglass under severe strain.

8. *On outboard hulls make sure that a metal engine mounting plate is present.* Fiberglass/polyester, not being as malleable as metal, would soon wear under the motor clamps and cause the motor to loosen.

9. *Avoid the "sexy" glitter finishes if you anticipate rough usage.* These finishes, although very attractive, are considerably harder to repair (and sometimes impossible) in comparison to solid color finishes. All boats sooner or later will be subjected to damage which would necessitate major or minor gel coat repairs.

10. *Check the hull-to-deck fastenings.* These should be properly fastened nuts and bolts or heavy duty "pop" rivets. Light "pop" rivets, and sometimes even staples, have been used, indicating a very inferior product.

11. *Check gel coat cure.* If possible, take a small amount of acetone on your fingertip and rub it onto the exterior gel coat—particularly colors other than white. If the boat seller does not have apoplexy and the surface does not become tacky, or some pigment does not come off on your fingertip, you have a properly cured gel coat. If your fingertip does become stained with the pigment or the surface does get tacky, it indicates an improperly cured gel coat and that boat should be avoided like the bubonic plague. Although this condition is rare, it does occasionally happen and, embarrassingly enough, it once happened to me—too late, of course.

12. *Check the inside of the hull for evidence of either woven cloth or woven roving.* On a hand lay-up hull the weave pattern is readily visible on the inside and this indicates that the proper type of reinforcement has been used. Beware of the hand lay-up boat that shows no evidence of woven reinforcement, as that boat was probably made using all matt or chopped glass and the glass content would be insufficient to yield maximum strength. On large cruiser hulls it is customary to use every second ply of woven roving with the alternate plies being matt or chopped glass. This is good construction.

13. *Check for "star" or "spider web" cracks in the gel coat.* This could indicate a gel coat that is too thick, a gel coat that is too rigid, or a laminate that is too thin.

14. *Check for a residual almondlike odor on the interior surfaces, particularly in the cabin of a cruiser.* Such an odor is caused by the manufacturer's failure to use a surfacing type of resin on the interior portion of his lay-up. Although this is not disastrous, it is annoying to have to expel this odor every time after the cabin has been closed for an extended period. The odor will eventually disappear, but it may take a year or two to do so.

15. *Check for a coat of paint over the gel coat.* Gel coats are meant to be the permanent exterior surface of the boat hull and superstructure. A coating of paint over the entire surface usually indicates an inferior gel coat, excessive handling, or shipping damage, or a boat manufacturer who chooses not to use a pigmented gel coat. The acetone trick will work well on most conventional paints (not the epoxies) if you are willing to risk another case of apoplexy.

The foregoing precautions may lead the reader to suspect that I am dead-set against fiberglass/polyester boats. Contrarily, I am not, and I would have no other type. These problems are very much in the minority but they do exist, and not only with small unknown companies. Twenty years of experience as a boat owner, polyester compounder, troubleshooter, raw material supplier, fabricator and many-times negotiator, have taught me to thoroughly inspect my future purchases. Even the most prominent companies are known to "flub" occasionally.

24

REPAIRING FIBERGLASS AUTO BODIES
AND OTHER UNITS

Each day, new fiberglass items are being introduced into the market place. Items which were customarily made with metal and other materials are being replaced with fiberglass/polyester components. These include snowmobile bodies, motorcycle components, outboard motor cowlings, luggage racks, furniture, camping equipment, marine accessories, trailers, and so many others that it would take several pages to list them all.

Fiberglass reinforced items are very durable, but by no means indestructible, and sooner or later they all will require maintenance or repair.

The directions for boat repairs will apply to these other items with few exceptions or modifications.

The major difference between boat hulls and fiberglass auto bodies is that the auto bodies do not employ a pigmented gel coat as the final color finish. Instead, they are painted with conventional auto finishes such as enamels or lacquers. Many of the aforementioned items are finished in the same manner and it is easy to determine if a gel coat has been used.

Paint finishes are much thinner than pigmented gel coats (1—2 mils vs. 10—20 mils), and can easily be scraped off the surface with the blade of a penknife.

Some pressure-molded fiberglass components, such as certain outboard motor cowls, have the color molded throughout the entire thickness of the laminate. These can easily be recognized by their fiberglass texture on the surface which is not as smooth and glossy as a gel coat or painted surface.

First, you must determine whether or not a gel coat has been used. If a gel coat has been used, you proceed with the repair exactly as if you were repairing a boat hull.

If a gel coat has not been used (as with an auto body), a different finishing procedure will be followed.

Structural repairs are the same on all fiberglass/polyester items and these repairs should be made in accordance with the directions for boat repairs.

Final finishing will follow the procedures normally used on conventional auto-finishing techniques. Once the structural repair is completed, the exterior surface should be thoroughly sanded with medium or fine abrasive paper to present a clean surface, and to remove the existing paint film on the adjacent surface.

All dents, low spots, nicks or gouges should then be filled with a conventional auto body filling compound, following the instructions on the can. Once cured, the surface should be resanded with fine paper and re-examined. If any flaws exist, the procedure should be repeated until you are satisfied that the surface is perfect and ready to receive the paint coating.

Corvette with a complete polyester fiberglass body.

Mask off the adjacent areas and sand again with very fine paper (400 grit wet dry) to remove all scratches and finger marks. The paper can be used wet or dry. If used wet, the water should be allowed to thoroughly evaporate and the surface should be thoroughly dry.

Dust the area with a clean dry cloth and do not touch the surface with your fingers or hands. Skin oil can cause paints to crawl.

From there on you follow conventional auto-painting procedures.

It is essential that a dust-free area be available for fine spray work, as small particles of dust in or under a thin paint film will be very predominant.

Spray on a coat of primer or primer/surfacer and allow it to dry. After it is thoroughly dry, wet-sand with 400 and 600 paper to present a perfectly smooth scratch-free surface. If any flaws exist, repeat the procedure.

Wipe the dry primed surface with an automotive "tac" cloth which will remove all traces of dust.

Immediately spray the area with a thin coat of automotive refinishing sealer which is a clear lacquer, non-sanding type. If you are going to use an acrylic enamel as the final coat, this sealer should be an acrylic sealer.

Then the final coat of paint or lacquer is applied following the instructions of the specific manufacturer.

If a lacquer is used as the final finish, it should be allowed to dry for at least eight hours and rubbed with a conventional lacquer rubbing compound to bring out the final luster.

For other fiberglass surfaces where a gel coat has not been used, the entire surface should be sanded to a uniform surface texture, and the auto-finishing procedures followed for a final finish, unless a polyester finish is desired. In this case, follow the procedures outlined in the boating sections.

25.

MONEY-SAVING HINTS

There are many ways to avoid wasting money in the fiberglass/polyester trade. Here are a few of them:

Scrap Glass. Small pieces, trim-offs and scraps which you have paid for, need not be discarded. They can be used just as effectively as the large pieces by overlapping in patches. When using small pieces, lap at least two inches and this will be as strong as one continuous piece—in fact, stronger. If they are not needed for your current repair, store them in a plastic bag, as they will virtually keep forever.

Resin Usage. Never catalyze more resin than you will require, as once it is catalyzed it will harden. Unless you need a lot of paperweights, it will be wasted. Rather than mix one large batch and throw away the portion which was not required, it is always better to mix in small amounts to complete the repair.

Resin Storage. Normally polyester resins have a shelf life of six months to one year at normal room temperature. After this, they proceed to polymerize and become useless—eventually solidifying.

(a) Always store resin in the coolest possible location, for ambient heat acts like a mild catalyst and will eventually set up the resin. If, for example, you could keep it in a refrigerator, it would last for many years.

(b) Never store resins for prolonged periods of time in clear glass or plastic containers, as ultraviolet rays likewise act as a mild catalyst, and will cause the resin to harden prematurely. If stored in such containers, keep in a dark location.

(c) Avoid storing a small amount of resin in a large can, as excess air (with its moisture) likewise acts as a mild catalyst and will eventually do you in. Keep as much air out as possible by storing the resin in smaller sealed cans. One method of precluding air is to float a circular piece of plastic wrap or wax paper on top of the resin in the can.

Buying Resins. In the industry, polyester resins are sold by the pound, but when they are repackaged, they are retailed by the quart or gallon. Check the *net* weight of the resin in a can. A full quart of resin should weigh 2¼ lbs. If you buy a "quart" weighing 2 lbs., you are not getting a full quart. If you shop, you will sometimes find that the "quart" with the lowest price is not the best buy, after all. If you anticipate quantity, it is always much cheaper to buy by the gallon or five-gallon pail.

Fiberglass. Fiberglass materials are sold within the industry by the pound and retailed by the square foot or square yard. Check the weight of the materials if at all possible. Woven fiberglass fabric (boat cloth) is generally available in 7 oz. and 10 oz. weights (7 or 10 oz. per sq. yd.). Even though the 10 oz. material is the standard, some shrewd operators sell the 7 oz. at a "discount." It takes an expert to tell the difference by sight or feel, and if you are buying 7 oz. cloth, comparing it with 10 oz., you are probably paying a lot more than it is worth. The same holds true for roving and particularly matt.

For the boat owner making an occasional repair the difference is not that significant, but for the serious aspirant to the profession, it can mean the difference between profit and loss.

Resin Coverage—10 oz. fiberglass boat cloth: Figure 1 qt. resin for 1 sq. yd. total—for the three coats to laminate to wood (primer, saturation coat, and top coat). For saturation alone (as in a composite laminate) one-half of this amount.

¾ oz. fiberglass matt—1 gal. resin will saturate 36 sq. ft. of matt (4 sq. yds.) and will produce a laminate about 1/32″ or .030″ weighing 1.70 lbs. per sq. yd.

24 oz. woven roving—1 gal. resin will saturate 33 sq. ft. of woven roving (3.66 yds.) and produce a laminate 3/64″ or .050″ weighing 3.17 lbs. per sq. yd.

Cleanup. As previously mentioned in Chapter 6, on cleanup, use the three-covered-can system for cleaning brushes. If you let resin harden in a brush, the only alternative is to sharpen the hardened bristles on a grindstone and convert it into a chisel. There is no known solvent for cured polyesters! If you are going to use paint rollers for large applications, buy mohair short-napped rollers. Also invest in an inexpensive half-moon type roller scraper to remove the excess resin from the roller before cleaning it in acetone. After cleaning the roller cover, remove it from the roller handle and give both a final separate cleaning.

Acetone. There is no more efficient cleaning agent for polyesters than acetone. Buying acetone in small quantities can be expensive. If you anticipate commercial activity where you will use large quantities of acetone, check your local chemical supply houses for five-gallon rates. Some marine distributors will order acetone, as well as resins, in five-gallon quantities for you.

Sanding a Tacky Surface. There are occasions when a "goof" occurs and you may end up with a tacky surface which you will want to sand. One solution is to apply another coat of non-air-inhibited resin and let it cure before sanding. Another method is to remove the tacky portion with a "Red Devil" hook type paint scraper. The gummy residue is easily removed from the blade and this will save considerable sandpaper. This technique is also particularly useful for removing bumps or lumps from an air-inhibited lay-up, before proceeding to apply more fiberglass and resin.

Recovering Wet Dry Paper. Wet dry paper has a very hard abrasive coating which does not dull easily. If it becomes clogged with dust or slurry, soak it in water and use a brush to remove the residue. In this manner it can be recovered and stored for future use.

26.

HOW FIBERGLASS BOATS ARE MADE

Although this book does not go into detail on fiberglass reinforced plastics manufacturing procedures, it is useful for the craftsman to understand just how these products are made.

The Plug. The first step in producing a fiberglass piece (a boat hull for example) is to make the male "plug." This plug is a full-scale model of the piece ultimately to be produced. The plug can be made of metal, plaster, or fiberglass/polyester-covered wood. In the case of wood, a wooden hull is constructed paying attention only to the outside surface. Once the hull is finished, it is laminated with fiberglass fabric and polyester resins. Many coats of surfacing resin are applied, and sanded between coats. When the exterior surface is perfect in respect to contour and surface texture, the entire surface is wet dry sanded and highly polished with buffing and polishing compounds. Every minute scratch or flaw is removed, because when the female mold is made from the plug, any imperfection in the surface will be reproduced (mirrored) in the female mold surface.

When using plaster as a plug material, it is allowed to dry thoroughly, and is given many coats of automotive type filler sealer, each sanded between coats. The plaster must be completely sealed to prevent the succeeding coats of mold gel coat from adhering.

After the plug is finished to perfection, several coats of parting agent (separating agents) are applied to prevent sticking.

Parting agents are available in wax or liquid form, and in many instances they are used in conjunction with each other on the plug. It is most essential that the entire surface be completely coated with parting agent, as one small "skip" will allow the succeeding mold to stick to the plug.

The Mold. This is generally made of fiberglass and polyester, and when cast over the male plug, it will be "female" in nature with a smooth interior.

First, a liberal coat of pigmented gel coat (and sometimes two coats) is applied and allowed to gel. Following this, one or two layers of matt are applied and saturated with clear lay-up resin; then fiberglass cloth, followed by alternate layers of matt and woven roving—all saturated with resin. After the desired thickness is achieved, wooden or metal stiffeners are sometimes added to keep the mold from distorting or unduly flexing when removed from the plug.

After this mold laminate is completely cured, it is pulled from the plug. Sometimes air or water pressure is used, or the mold can be carefully pried from the plug.

This is "the moment of truth" which causes ulcers for all involved; for if the parting agent or gel coat were not properly applied, the pieces could stick together and ruin both the plug and the mold.

Once the mold is removed from the plug, the mold is used to produce the boat hulls, and the plug is put aside to use in making other molds, if required.

If small mold imperfections exist, such as air bubbles between the gel coat and first ply of glass, these are carefully repaired by the procedures outlined in this book, and the mold is then ready for production.

The Production Pieces. The same basic procedure is followed to make the hulls as was used to make the mold. Parting agent is applied, followed by pigmented gel coat, then by fiberglass and lay-up resin to build up to the desired thickness. When the piece is removed from the female mold, it will have a smooth shiny exterior surface, with a coarse fiberglass texture on the interior. The interior is usually finished with a surface coat or paint and generally will remain coarse in texture.

This chapter describes only the basic hand lay-up techniques, and does not attempt to cover more complex methods.

BEGINNER'S GLOSSARY FOR POLYESTER AND FIBERGLASS

A. General:

1. *Lay-Up.* A technique of molding the reinforcement (glass) and liquid plastic in a mold to produce an item. Also referred to as a laminate.

2. *Mil.* A measurement equal to one-thousandth of one inch. Generally used to measure the diameter of glass filaments or the thickness of an applied coating.

3. *Reinforced Plastic.* A combination of plastic and reinforcement filaments to produce optimum strength—generally, but not limited to fiberglass and polyester resins.

4. *Reinforcement.* Generally fiberglass filaments in either woven or matt form to provide high tensile strength when combined with plastics. Other materials such as asbestos, nylon, and sisal are also used.

5. *Thermoplastic.* A solid material which liquefies by the application of heat and rehardens at room temperatures. Generally can be softened or formed by the application of mild heat.

6. *Thermosetting Plastic.* A liquid plastic that cures (or hardens) with the application of heat—either direct or through chemical reaction. Cannot be reliquefied.

B. Reinforcement:

1. *Binder.* Generally used to hold fiberglass matt together in a compressed state similar to felt, for dry handling purposes. The binder is usually dissolved by the subsequent application of resin to allow it to configurate to the mold surface during the molding process.

2. *Chopped Strand.* Continuous glass roving chopped into uniform lengths, usually from ¼″ to 3″ long. Lengths under 1/8″ are called milled fibers.

3. *Continuous Filament Strand.* A single filament of glass with a small diameter.

4. *End.* A strand of roving consisting of a given number of filaments.

5. *Fiberglas*®*.* Fibers made from glass; glass fiber forms include cloth, yarn, matt, milled fibers, chopped strands, roving, woven roving.

6. *Filament.* A single thread of fiberglass in continuous form.

7. *Finishes.* On woven fiberglass fabrics, various types of finishes (such as chrome and Volan) are available to promote better penetration of the resin into the cloth. These finishes cause the cloth to be shiny in appearance. Dull finished cloth should be avoided as it is inferior for "wetting out" purposes.

8. *Glass Content.* The amount of fiberglass, by weight, in proportion to the amount of resin in the finished piece. Example: A finished piece weighing 100 lbs., containing 40 lbs. of glass reinforcement and 60 lbs. of resin, has a glass content of 40%.

9. *Matt.* Randomly distributed strands of chopped fibers pressed together in felt form and held together by a binder.

10. *Roving (Filament Winding).* Bundles of continuous filaments either as untwisted strands or as twisted yarns.

11. *Spray Up.* A method used to produce fiberglass reinforced items by simultaneously spraying chopped roving and resins onto the mold surface. The wetted fibers are then rolled into a compressed state and allowed to cure without external pressure. Laminates of 25—35% glass are produced resulting in weaker parts in comparison to woven fabric or roving laminates.

12. *Woven Cloth.* A cloth woven from fiberglass filaments. It is used where high strength is important and good drape is required.

13. *Woven Roving Fabric.* Heavy fabric woven from continuous strands of roving. It has good drape, wets out readily, is intermediately priced, and offers excellent tensile strength.

C. Plastic Resins:

1. *Acetone.* One of the most efficient solvents used for tool and hand cleaning. It should not (contrary to some practices) be used to thin polyester because entrapment of this material within the cured polyester would degrade the general characteristics of the cured piece. It has a very low flash point and is extremely flammable.

2. *Air Inhibition (sometimes Surface Inhibition).* A resin that cures throughout its thickness except for the uppermost surface which is exposed to air. During curing, the air in contact with this surface retards the surface cure causing the uppermost surface to remain "tacky." This permits a true molecular bond to take place between this surface and subsequent applications of polyester. Surface-inhibited resins cannot be readily sanded as they would clog the sandpaper.

3. *Back-Up Coat.* A dark pigmented gel coat applied over the white gel coat to provide contrast so that air bubbles can be seen readily when making the fiberglass lay-up.

4. *Cabosil®.* An ultra lightweight filler commonly used to make a liquid plastic thixotropic. Generally added in proportions of 1% to 3% (by weight).

5. *Catalyst (also called Hardener).* A peroxide material, usually a clear liquid, which is added to the promoted resin in small quantities (usually 1% by weight—roughly ½ oz. or 10 cc. per qt. of resin) to effect a cure.

6. *Chemical Inhibitor.* A substance which slows down or prevents

the polyester from curing. Oil, water, wood resin, and paint thinners are typical inhibitors which would retard or prevent the cure of general purpose polyesters.

7. *Crazing.* Cracking generally due to excessive exotherm being developed in the piece while curing.

8. *Cure Time.* The time it takes for the lay-up to achieve a hard cure suitable for removing the piece from the mold and for permitting subsequent handling.

9. *Epoxy Resins.* Also liquid thermosetting plastics noted for their greater tensile strength and adhesion to nonporous substrates. They are considerably more expensive than polyesters and are consequently limited in boat use, where the lower priced polyesters do a satisfactory job. They are also generally more difficult to work with from a toxicity and curing standpoint.

10. *Exotherm.* The internal heat generated within the resin due to polymerization.

11. *Fillers.* Powdered materials such as clays, talc, mica, marble dust, etc., which are mixed with the liquid polyesters to extend their bulk and thicken the material. Various filler compounds are used to produce seam fillers, auto body patching compounds, dent and nick fillers, casting compounds, etc.

12. *Gel Coat.* A semi-thixotropic, air-inhibited, usually pigmented resin which is applied to the mold surface (after parting agent) upon which the subsequent fiberglass lay-up is made. When the piece is removed from the mold, the gel coat represents the final outside finish of the article.

13. *Gel Time.* The time it takes for the polyester to leave its liquid state and achieve a gelatinous consistency.

14. *High Temperature Surface Inhibition.* This occurs when surfacing resins are applied to hot surfaces (over $100°$ F.). Such high temperatures cause the surfacing additive to melt, rendering it ineffective and causing a tacky surface to exist in the presence of air. This does not affect the under-cure, but only the uppermost surface. Surfacing resins should be applied in the shade.

15. *Lay-up Resin.* A slightly thixotropic clear promoted resin designed for good fiberglass saturation. It is generally air-inhibited to permit a molecular bond to exist between coats, even if the resin cures between coats.

16. *Pigments.* Pastes made from combining powdered color pigments with a liquid vehicle. The pigments themselves can be either organic or inorganic, with the inorganic pigments exhibiting superior light stability and permanence. Organic pigments have a tendency to fade and deteriorate in the sunlight. Only sufficient pigment should be added to the resin to accomplish opacity, as overpigmentation could cause total inhibition due to a superfluous amount of the vehicle involved.

17. *Polyester Resins.* Liquid thermosetting plastics which cure into a solid mass by the application of physical heat and/or chemical heat. They are noted for their excellent penetration qualities, weathering resistance, and general chemical resistance. They are used primarily in conjunction with fiberglass reinforcement to manufacture such items as boat hulls, auto bodies, etc.

18. *Polymerization.* A process where the molecules of the resin cross-link to change from a liquid to a solid.

19. *Post Cure.* The time it takes for the piece to achieve its ultimate hardness and chemical resistance; usually two weeks at room temperature, although this time can be greatly reduced by the application of heat.

20. *Pot Life.* The working time of a resin (while it is still liquid) after the catalyst has been added.

21. *Preaccelerated (also Prepromoted).* Used to describe a polyester which has had the accelerator added by the manufacturer or processor.

22. *Promoter.* Also called accelerator. Usually a liquid metal compound added to the polyester in small quantities to react with the subsequently added catalyst causing a "chemical heat" to be generated, thereby causing the polyester to cure into a solid mass. The promoter can be added to the resin by the manufacturer and will not affect the shelf life of the resin. The most common type is a cobalt which is deep purple in color, and is generally added to the resin at a proportion of ½ of one percent by weight. Cobalts are available in various strength compounds for extremely fast cures.

23. *Styrene.* One of the more common monomers used to thin (reduce the viscosity) of polyesters. This water-thin clear liquid is also 100% solids and cross-links with the polyester during curing, thereby maintaining the 100% solids integrity of the polyester resin.

24. *Surface Coating Resins (sometimes referred to as Surfacing Gel Coats or Non-Air-Inhibited Resins).* Resins which have a waxy additive which, when the resin is applied, prevents the air from inhibiting the uppermost surface. Such resins cure "tack-free" and can be readily sanded without clogging the sandpaper. They must be sanded to break the surface to insure a molecular bond if they are to be recoated.

25. *Surfacing Additive.* A clear liquid containing the waxy additives which are mixed with the liquid polyesters in small quantities (usually 1% by weight) to prevent air inhibition. Materials and mixing temperatures should exceed 70° F.

26. *Thixotropic.* A resin which has been modified with ultra lightweight fillers to prevent running or sagging on vertical or inclined surfaces. Can be compared to whipped cream, which is a relative solid when not in motion and a relative fluid when in motion.

27. *Total Inhibition.* A resin which will not cure, or which achieves

only a partial cure throughout its entire thickness due to improper mixing, low temperatures, or chemical contaminants.

28. *Trim Time.* The time it takes for the lay-up to achieve a rubbery consistency, which permits knife-trimming the excess material from the mold edges.

29. *Viscosity.* The term used to describe the thickness (flow rate) of a liquid. Can be compared to viscosities used in motor oils such as "high" ("STP"—about 80), versus "low" (# 10 motor oil).

30. *100% Solids.* A term applied to plastics indicating that they contain no evaporative solvents, as such, and will cure in thin films or mass without the evaporation of solvents. (Paints dry by the evaporation of solvents.)

31. *15° Rule.* For each 15°F. rise in temperature over the normal (considered at 75°F.) the pot life and cure time will be halved. Conversely for each 15° decrease in temperature, the pot life and cure time will be doubled. Ambient, materials, and surface temperatures must be taken into consideration.

D. Lay-up Terminology:

1. *Mold.* This is the piece into which the fiberglass and polyester is layed up to produce the finished product. The mold is usually made of fiberglass and polyester and should have a perfect interior finish, as any flaw will be reproduced in all subsequent pieces.

2. *Mold Release (sometimes called Parting Agent).* A material applied to the mold surface to prevent sticking of the piece. It can be a paste type wax or a liquid release agent. On new molds a combination of the two can be used to insure good release.

3. *Plug.* A model of the piece to be produced. Usually made of wood, wood and fiberglass, plaster, etc. It is from this plug that the fiberglass mold is made.

4. *Prune Skinning.* An undesirable texture found in the gel coat after the piece is removed from the mold. It is generally due to the gel coat being applied too thin, or otherwise totally inhibited. The subsequent lay-up resins will swell the gel coat and cause it to prematurely release from the mold while the lay-up resin is still in a liquid form.

5. *Undercut.* Female depressions in the mold. Split molds are necessary when undercuts are present in order to remove the piece with its projections from the mold.

Fiberglas® is a registered trademark of Owens-Corning Fiberglas Corp.
Cabosil® is a registered trademark of Cabot Corp.